I Will Build a

Barn

A History of Ponca Hills Farm

By Vicki Krecek

"My fondest personal memory was galloping wonderful, talented, Pride, across the high meadow on that lovely deep soil with no rocks, on a beautiful summer day and thinking, 'This is as good as it gets.'"

-Philip Durbrow

Dedication

To Allan and Ann Mactier for having the dream, the vision and the courage to create a place and an organization where hundreds of children and adults have learned to ride and care for horses for the last fifty years. Ponca Hills Farm and the Mactiers' formula has included working hard, learning from the best, and always, having fun.

And to their daughter, Jan Moriarty, for continuing their dream.

"Most of us didn't realize while we were taking advantage of the first-class facilities and instructors at Ponca Hill Equestrian Center, what an impact it would have on our lives, our children's lives, and our grandchildren's lives. We came to count on all that was offered, never considering all that went in to making our dreams come true. We would be remiss to not extend a sincere 'thank you' to the J. Allan Mactier family, especially Ann and Jan, for their generosity that has meant so much to so many. It may be late; but it is sincere, THANK YOU…" *Merrilee Hansen, Former Boarder/Pony Club Mom*

Acknowledgements

There is no way to capture all of the people, the horses, or the events of Ponca Hills Farm over its 50 years. Instead, we have tried to present a rough history, much of it a compilation of memories of the boarders, managers, and instructors, as well as members of the Ponca Pony Club and North Hills Hunt.

First, our thanks to Merrilee Hansen, who started riding at Ponca just out of college, and raised two Ponca Pony Club members. Merrilee not only helped put together the Ponca Pony Club history, she spent hours editing and giving helpful suggestions. We wouldn't have had a book without her.

Special thanks to April Goettle, graphic designer and horsewoman, who took on the layout and editing of pictures; and to Pat Waters, editor extraordinaire, for final editing. Thank you to Robyn Eden for her vision for the project and to her and Legacy Productions, for the initial outline and compilation of historic data.

Thanks to Carole, Glenn and Brent Cudmore, Mike Blose, Nancy Zandbergen Wilson (who even mailed us her Pony Club scrapbook), Pat, Kirsten and Kirk Wagner, Merrilee, Leslie and Sara Hansen, Sherma and Krystal Seitzinger, Paula and Lowell Smalley, Dan McGuire, Susie Gordon Matheson, Linda Gordman, Margie Hoffmaster and her daughter Elizabeth, Jean Rude, Gary Young, Phil Durbrow, Tom Ordway, Archie Cox, and so many others who shared their memories.

And most especially thanks to Jan Mactier Moriarty for her wonderful recollections, thousands of pictures, and determination to get this book completed and available to those we call Ponca Hills Farm Family!

A Note from Jan Mactier Moriarty

With this project has come many more memories, reintroductions, and rediscoveries of so many Ponca family and friends. The legacy of my parents was to have Ponca Hills Farm be inclusive rather than exclusive; a place where all are welcome; and a place where there is always more to learn. So many have stepped in, sharing their time, their knowledge, and their expertise, and their love of horses. Ponca is the sum of all of those people - boarders, students, instructors, and farm hands.

We wish we had remembered to keep everyone's name and addresses over the 55+ years, so we could know where they live and whether horses are still a part of their lives. Hopefully this book will stimulate some of your memories of horses, friends and of Ponca Hills Farm. We invite you to share your memories with us, online, or better yet, just stop by to say "Hello." We hope your good times, good friends and good memories of Ponca will last forever.

Our thanks to Vicki Krecek for cheerfully taking on this project. Her energy, enthusiasm and dedication and ideas are beyond measure.

Cover Picture - Sparrow, decorated for the final day of summer camp, is proudly shown over ground poles by Hudson Chapman during the camp show. Parents watch proudly from the bank on the outside arena. Sparrow is the mother of Birdie and Lamb Chop, all Connemara ponies owned by Ponca Hills Farm.

Table of Contents

Preface
Nebraska Heritage

Figure 1. Allan's father, Grandpa Mac, rode his horse to work at "the World's Largest Livestock Market" where he built a well-known livestock commission firm.

Agriculture is big business in Nebraska and the Great Plains. From the earliest settling of the west, this area has grown and prospered because of its ability to expand production and processing of food for regional, and later world-wide, markets. Today, Nebraska and Iowa rank among the top states in the production and export of both crops and livestock. The families who came to this area established homesteads and communities with a heavy emphasis on stewardship of the land. Nebraska's first settlers and agricultural leaders have always put a priority on support of education.

The Mactier and Dickinson families are examples of that heritage. Both families were key participants in businesses that processed crops and livestock for international markets. Allan Mactier became an important contributor to Nebraska's leadership in the food processing industry while Ann Dickinson Mactier made lasting contributions to education in both Omaha and Nebraska.

In addition to their notable careers, Allan and Ann Mactier turned their love of land and of horses to establishing an outstanding equestrian center and nature preserve in Omaha's northern hills.

In the first decade after returning from service in World War II, Allan renewed old friendships and developed new ones among men who had also served in the war and who loved horses. They frequently gathered to ride and, as their families and businesses grew, so did their interest in promoting their love of riding and the outdoors. They began to share their passion with others and to educate young people in the care and discipline of riding horses.

In 1964 this group of friends founded the North Hills Hunt and Mactiers purchased property and built a barn. With so much collective experience in the military, it is not surprising there was an emphasis on learning correct and safe ways of handling 1,000 to 1,200-pound animals.

Since 1965, Ponca Hills Farm has continued that discipline in the education of young people who want to learn to ride and care for horses and has placed emphasis on preservation of the land and trails in the hills along the Missouri River.

The Founders

Figure 1. Allan grew up near the Field Club, a few blocks from the Stockyards stable. He kept a pony in his back yard.

J. Allan Mactier

J. Allan Mactier was born in Arlington, NE on May 21, 1922. His father, Allan Mactier, a "Grandpa Mac" to J. Allan's children, was one of 13 children, nine of whom lived. At age 13, Mac left home "because there were too many mouths to feed". He had achieved an 8th grade education at Elk City, NE and went to Omaha to work at the stockyards. The Union Stockyards was rapidly growing and competed with Chicago for the title of World's Largest Livestock Market and Meat Packing Plant. Grandpa Mac founded Mactier Bros. and built it into a well-known livestock commission firm. For many years it was the largest livestock commission firm in the country. Allan grew up in the Field Club neighborhood. As a child, he had a pony which was kept in his back yard. (His Dad would ride his horse from the Stockyards stable, near 36th and Martha, to work at the stockyards.) As a child, Allan would go to Ak-Sar-Ben racetrack to watch the horses being exercised, inspiring a life-long interest in horses and horse racing. At Omaha

Central High School, he was editor of the Central High Register. There he met Ann Dickinson, also a Register editor.

Allan graduated from the University of Michigan with a degree in economics. There he was head of the Navy ROTC and received a commission in the U.S. Navy. After graduating early, Allan was commissioned in the Navy submarine service in WWII. He and Ann married the same day, February 26, 1944 at his fraternity house on the University of Michigan campus. Ann and Allan then went to New Castle, CT for him to attend submarine school.

When they returned to Omaha, Allan went to work selling flour for his father-in-law Robert Dickinson. Dickinson was instrumental in consolidating flour mills under the name Nebraska Consolidated Mills.

In the next ten years, Allan, who had taken (but never finished) a correspondence course in flour milling at the University of Michigan, worked his way up, becoming executive vice-president. Nebraska Consolidated Mills was known for Mother's Best Flour. Allan worked to expand the reach of the company. He became known as the man who put angel food cake mix into a box, launching Duncan Hines cake mixes in 1951.

Daughter Jan recalls that she and her brothers would go to her Dad's office on Saturdays to tour the plant and visit the test kitchens to taste the cake, which, Jan said, tasted better than the other brands. The secret was the two-step process. She remembers meeting the "real" Duncan Hines, known for "three fingers of bourbon and many watches on his arm." Allan became the third president of the company in 1954. Nebraska Consolidated Mills grew into a major food company and was renamed ConAgra in 1971. At one point, Allan built a flour mill called Molinos De Puerto Rico. For a while, it made up a third of the business.

When the Duncan Hines cake mix division was sold in the mid-fifties, Allan was offered a job in Cincinnati following the sale, but Ann said "NO" and Allan replied that he "would rather be my own boss." By then they owned property on North Post Road. Allan retired from ConAgra in 1974.

Not only did Allan contribute to building a major Omaha corporation, he was also a civic leader on the executive committee of the Greater Omaha Chamber of Commerce and many others non-profit organizations including United Way, March of Dimes, and the Ak-Sar-Ben Governors, an organization that led efforts to restore the Orpheum Theater as a performing arts venue. J. Allan Mactier died on February 25, 2005.

Ann Dickinson Mactier

Figure 2. Ann's mother, Carrie Clark Dickinson(right) in Ravenna, NE1913.

Ann Dickinson was born June 29, 1922 in Ravenna, NE, the daughter of Robert Smith Dickinson and Carrie (Clark) Dickinson.

Carrie came to Nebraska from New York and taught school in Ravenna. Ann's father Robert Dickinson, or "Grandpa Dick" to his grandchildren, attended Doane College in Crete, NE graduating in 1910 with an accounting degree and took a job as bookkeeper, office boy and janitor at the Ravenna flour mill, the start of a 60-year career in flour milling. He worked his way up in the company and earned a notable reputation when he helped orchestrate the merger of several flour mills in the Grand Island area. In 1919, he helped found and was named Vice President of Nebraska Consolidated Mills. He became President in 1936 and Chairman in 1956 and was a key figure in the company's evolution from a small local business into what later became ConAgra, an international corporation. He served as a Director of the Millers' National Federation for eighteen years and was on its executive committee for ten years. In 1943, he became the second president of the Nebraska Grain Improvement Association, and initiated programs to improve the quality of the variety of wheat produced in the state. Other states then copied Nebraska's methods.

Daughter Ann had an early love of horses. She attended Columbian Grade School and later Central High School in Omaha where she met Allan Mactier. She attended Northwestern University in Chicago and would frequently visit Allan in Ann Arbor. Ann graduated from Northwestern in 1944 and later added a master's degree in arts from the University of Omaha (1963) and an Honorary Doctor of Education from the University of Nebraska-Lincoln in 2005.

Ann Dickinson Mactier made a significant mark on the Omaha community with a lifelong interest in the education of young people. For several decades she was elected to education leadership positions and was a driving force influencing how beginning reading was taught to children, earning the nickname "The Reading Lady." She is a founder of the Phoenix Academy. A private school, Phoenix Academy educates students with learning differences and helps them realize their full academic potential and become successful in school and in life. The school uses a phonics-based education mode, focusing on reading, spelling, writing and math. Over 80% of the students receive financial aid, 49% are minorities, 50% come from single parent households and

33% have expenses covered by tuition. No student is turned away because they can't pay.

She served as Vice President of the Nebraska State Board of Education. She was a member of the Omaha Public Schools Board of Education from 1983 to 1998. She is credited by many for helping establish Omaha North High School as a computer magnet school, which continues to attract students from all over the metro area.

In addition, Ann was active in the community, including a member of the Junior League of Omaha, the executive committee for the Riverfront Development Corporation (1973 to 1979), and the steering committee for the Council Urban Boards of Education (1996-98). She served on the Board of Directors for the Council Great City Schools (1984-89), was the community coordinator for the College of Fine Arts for the University of Nebraska (1974-75) and founder and president of the Florence Arts Council.

Ann was owner/manager of Ponca Hills Riding Academy from 1966 until 1973 and was inducted into the Central High School Hall of Fame on October 3, 2002. She and Allan raised three children: James Allan Mactier II (Jim), Judith Ann (Jan) and Robert Dickinson Mactier (Rob).

The Mactiers Discover Omaha's North Hills

After the war, Allan and Ann Mactier returned to Omaha. They lived near the Ak-Sar-Ben racetrack. Daughter Jan loved horses as a child and remembers going to Ak-Sar-Ben to watch the horses training and hear the trumpet signaling the start of the races.

Their good friend from Omaha Central High School, Nes Latenser and his parents, Alma and Frank Latenser lived in the Ponca

Hills area north of Omaha. (Frank, an architect with John Latenser and Sons Architects, designed the W. Dale Clark Library and the Northern Natural Gas Building.) Nes Latenser served in the Navy in WWII.

*Figure 3.*Jan with Mr. Red, at Auntie Alma's riding ring.

Allan and Ann spent much time at the Latensers' with their children, ice skating, tobogganing and sledding. Auntie Alma taught everyone to ride. The kids would ride the horse around the circular driveway until they could successfully stop, go and steer a horse. Lunch was always available, often "Some More" stew, named because everyone wanted some more! Their house was round and one wall in the kitchen was covered with names of people and marks showing how tall they were.

Ann and Allan loved the Ponca Hills area with its densely forested hills along the Missouri River. This area is rich with remnants and trails of the fur traders and of Indian settlements dating to the1400s. One still can find traces of the Omaha and Council Bluffs Grape Growers' vineyards, an industry that thrived in the 1800s.

Growers once said the climate along the river was similar to that of the Rhine Valley in Germany. The Missouri River creates constant moisture in the air resulting in a local climate that is cooler in summer and warmer in winter.

Radiating back from the river is hilly land dotted with steep ravines and dense forests. These are the Loess Hills, formed by centuries of topsoil blowing and settling along the river. The lack of bedrock in these hills provides great footing for horses and rich soil for growing plants, but development is difficult because the water table is at river

Figure 4. Ann and Allan kept their horses at their home on North Post Road. Allan is on Mr. Red, a Percheron Thoroughbred cross, and Ann on Lolly at Lowell Boomer's farm near Lincoln, 1963.

level, hundreds of feet below the hill tops. As a result, the Ponca Hills area developed later than the flatter, rolling land west and south of Omaha. These hills provide an environment for both abundant wildlife and for people who want to experience that wildlife. It includes remnants of the old fur trader's trail along Ponca Creek and hollows which were the lodges of the Native Americans in the 15th century. Here is an area that feels rural but is still just 20 minutes from downtown Omaha.

Ann's dream was to buy land and live in Ponca Hills. In 1956, Ann and Allan purchased land on North Post road. Ann's brother-in-law, Tom Keogh, designed the house they built on the property. They bought a horse, Van, from the Latensers for Allan. Van was soon joined by Ann's Misty Morning, and Lolly, a Saddlebred, in the Mactiers' back yard. Later, they added Jan's first pony, 20-year-old Dolly. Jan was nine.

Figure 5. Chuck wagon party at the home of Frank and Auntie Alma Latenser with big draft horses Dick and Bill. Allan is on board and the Governor of Puerto Rico is driving.

As a child, Jan was particularly fond of the Latensers' gentle work horses, Dick and Bill, who were broke to drive. "We had many a goulash supper at the Latensers' chuck wagon parties."

Jan, remembers riding horses from one home to another, mostly unencumbered by fences, but challenged by steep ravines. There were green open pastures and lush woods. Riding mostly bareback, she and her friends saw deer, coyote, foxes, bobcats, minks and eagles and hawks, all at close range.

One day Ann went to Hillside Stables, near 72nd and Dodge Street, to buy a used saddle for Allan. There she saw a German trainer, Hans Post, take a horse, Conawingo, over a jump. The horse was owned by Con Heafe. Post's day job was working as a butcher at Swift

Figure 6. Jan Mactier takes a jump at the cabbage patch, next to their home on North Post Road.

packing plant in the stockyards, but he spent all his spare time jumping horses. The Mactiers wanted to learn to jump also and engaged the services of Post to teach them. That was the start of a lifelong friendships with both Post and Con Heafe, and other horse lovers like Taylor and Alida Snow. Snows also lived in Omaha's North Hills and had horses on their acreage. Taylor was also interested in jumping and riding cross-country.

Their new home needed an outdoor jumping arena, so the Mactiers bought a cabbage field next to their house. They built some makeshift jumps out of barrels. When Ann and Allan tried to convince their horses to jump them, the horses refused. Jan tried the jumps with Dolly and sailed over all the obstacles.

Allan wanted a jumping horse. He went to Si Jaynes stable in Chicago to look at a horse, Invincible, doing a trial ride in his business

Figure 7. Ann Mactier with Misty Morning at Auntie Alma's.

suit. He purchased the horse and brought him home to Omaha. Si sent along a "bicycle chain bit" in case his daughter wanted to ride this very powerful, aggressive horse.

By the early 60s, Allan and Ann were thoroughly in love with the country lifestyle and its sporting and hospitality traditions. They also saw a real need for a place where those who wanted to learn to ride "English" could have the same opportunities as riders on the East Coast.

In the early 60s, the area was dominated by western riding. There were some Saddlebred and other saddle seat and driving enthusiasts, but hunters, jumpers, dressage and eventing were less well known and anyone interested had to go elsewhere to learn. Wanting to give their daughter the advantages of a proper equestrian as well as overall education, the Mactiers sent Jan to the Ethel Walker School in Connecticut in 1965. Walker's mission was to instill a lifelong love of learning while also offering young riders the opportunity to become good horsewomen. Jan was quickly becoming a good rider. "Mom was interested in the academics and curriculum. I was interested in their beautiful barn, indoor ring, extensive trails, and woods filled with wildflowers," Jan later remembered. "There was a horse show or two nearby but riding was considered an activity, like volleyball."

Let's Start a Fox Hunt

Figure 8. From left, Donovan Ketzler, Hans Post, Taylor Snow and Allan Mactier gather around Mactier's kitchen table for breakfast and planning to start a fox hunt.

Allan and Taylor Snow rode together on weekends and were often joined by Donovan Ketzler and Nancy Duhnke for rides which included jumping. This led them to want to try fox hunting. The closest hunts were the Mission Valley Hunt in Kansas City and the Fort Leavenworth Hunt. They loaded their horses and drove down to hunt near Kansas City several times a year. Since hunting season is from late fall to early spring, the weather was frequently bad, making the trips to these hunts challenging. After one particularly harrowing snowy drive, the group decided they should start a hunt in Omaha. They gathered for breakfast with a few others and discussed what was needed to start a hunt:

Taylor Snow said, "I will start a fox hunt."
Allan Mactier said, "I will build a barn."
And Hans Post said, "I will teach people to ride."

Fox hunting originally started in England in the 1600s and was often used as a training for cavalry officers, so there are strong military ties in its traditions. The North Hills Hunt was initiated in Omaha by men of military training whose first hunts included riding at the historic Fort Leavenworth whose membership included Generals George Stilwell, George Patton and Dwight Eisenhower. Given his military background and his love of the country life and land, it is not surprising that Allan Mactier found fox hunting appealing.

The founders and first members of North Hills Hunt were led by Taylor Snow. A well-known Omaha businessman, Snow was an attorney and owner of SnowCo, a manufacturer of farm machinery. Snow paid all the expenses until the Hunt could stand on its own, selected and purchased the hounds, built the kennels on his property, and arranged for permission to ride the land.

An officer in the U.S. Army at Fort Crook, Snow is described by everyone as "a gentleman first and foremost." Always very proper and well dressed, he had a lovely home in Ponca Hills and a beautiful barn with a brick floor. Both structures are still standing at the top of 51st Court. He and his wife Alida hosted many of the early Hunt "breakfasts." They rode and showed Tennessee Walking Horses extensively and had several world champions.

Snow was always available to help young people learn to tack up a horse or hitch a trailer. He encouraged new members, even loaning horses and equipment. Jan Mactier Moriarty remembers: "Tom Caniglia had his pony near Cooper Farm and rode bareback with a western bridle. Taylor asked him to join us and gave him an English bridle."

Hans Post was in the German Horse Cavalry and his role in the early days of the Hunt was as riding instructor. He often said, "When you and your horse are learning to ride it is better if one of you knows how already."

Donovan Ketzler owned the Dehner Company which had an international reputation for its custom-made English riding boots, military boots and specialized boots. He learned to ride with the U.S. Army Cavalry at Fort Omaha when he was only 12 years old. By age 14, he was an accomplished rider. He graduated from Central High School in 1942. As WWII involved the U.S., he enlisted in the horse cavalry and was sent to Fort Riley, Kansas. After basic training, he was made a drill sergeant and trained three classes of recruits in riding and weaponry before being sent to the China-Burma-India Theater.

Founder Nancy Duhnke was in her mid-30s with two young boys when the Hunt was formed. She rode as a young girl and took it up again when she moved to Omaha. She boarded her horse, Blueberry, at the "Henhouse," a barn in the North Hills leased by several early hunt members.

Founder Dr. Irwin "Dutch" Blose, an Omaha psychiatrist, raced Standardbred horses prior to developing a love for fox hunting. He was quite busy in his professional practice and was also raising five young children. Blose served in the Navy during WWII and was awarded the Navy Cross, the highest honor the Navy bestows. He often served as ring master for riding events. His son Mike is a farrier and has had a lifelong association with North Hills Hunt and Ponca Hills Farm, where he is the chief farrier today.

These are the individuals who built the North Hills Hunt. Because of their influence, the Hunt became an organization which focused on the education and development of young riders. At first these were the children of the founders and their friends. As more young people got involved, their parents became active participants in the social aspects of the hunt, often learning to ride themselves.

North Hills Hunt held its first "unofficial hunt" in late 1964 with just one couple of hounds. The riders left from the Mactiers' home on North Post Road. Both Allan Mactier and Ann rode that morning.

"The group headed south," Ketzler recalled. "We only went about 100 yards when another 50 yards in front of us, a fox jumped into our path. The hounds stopped. We stopped. The fox looked at us, and the hounds looked at the fox. All of a sudden, the fox took off with the hounds in hot pursuit. We couldn't follow them because it was heavily wooded in the gulley behind Allan's house. We called them and looked for them for three days but never found them."

After hunting, the group often went to Mactier's home for pancakes and to discuss the Hunt's future. These became regular breakfasts held at various members' homes. Jan Moriarty remembers at one breakfast the cook was asked to prepare a new, popular dish, which they pronounced "Keetchee Lorraine" They had never tried it, but everyone at the breakfast liked it. A meal after a foxhunt is always called a "hunt breakfast" no matter what the time of day.

I Will Build a Barn

It was Ann Mactier's childhood dream to have a horse, so she really was behind Allan's pledge to "build the barn." In 1964, Mactier purchased 60 acres of forests and pastures atop the highest hill in the county. It was on North 42nd Street, just north of Ponca Creek Road. The property included a farmhouse that still stands just west of the barn. They named it Ponca Hills Farm.

Mactier added additional acres in several purchases over the years. One purchase (which later became Hawk Wood Circle) was the location of the original cross-country and Steeplechase course. That land was later sold off as lots for homes adjacent to the farm. Another purchase was the "Voss" property (later sold to Mannheim Steamroller's Chip Davis.) The house and land where Jan and Mick Moriarty now live was an old farmhouse and former chicken and apple farm, built in 1867. Today Ponca Hills Farm occupies approximately 200 acres.

Huge amounts of dirt were brought in to create a level area for the barn. According to Jan Moriarty, the fill added over 40 feet to the hill and created a pad for the large barn, indoor arena, outdoor arena, and an outdoor jumping pasture. Fred Nance designed the barn, which was finished by 1965.

The barn was built in sections, starting with the east wing, then the west wing and a 100 x 200' indoor arena. At the time of its construction, it was reputed to be the largest indoor arena between Denver and Chicago. Mike Blose (lifetime rider, worker and then farrier at Ponca) recalls there were seventeen "straight" stalls in the east barn for the school horses. The center aisle stalls were added later.

Figure 9. Newly constructed barn at Ponca Hills Farm. The indoor arena was largest in the Midwest. The middle barn stalls were built later. A cross-country/jumping course was constructed north of the barn, in the north valley and apple orchard.

On move-in day, one of the first boarders, Gretchen Giltner, led the parade of horses from the Mactiers' home on North Post Road to the new facility. Mindy Nance, daughter of barn designer Fred Nance was also among the first boarders.

I Will Teach People to Ride - Ponca's Early Years

The Mactiers did not dream small. Their goal for Ponca Hills Farm was to build the best facility in the Midwest at the time. Allan focused on fox hunting, cross-country riding and, eventually, breeding Thoroughbreds. Ann focused on teaching people, starting with children, to ride and care for horses. Hans Post, a stockyards butcher who had said "I will teach people to ride," had moved to Des Moines before the barn was built. He was excited when offered a full-time job with horses. That left the "teaching people to ride" up to Ann, who was less interested in fox hunting, even though she handily jumped over three-foot fences.

Inspired by Post, Ann led Ponca Hills Farm to become the go-to place for English hunt seat riding, always insistent that top quality instruction be made available. She introduced programs that have made horsemen and women of hundreds of children. She started summer camps, Pony Club, lessons and clinics, all of which continue to educate riders today.

As soon as the barn was built, the Mactiers started acquiring horses, many of which came from Cal Miller in Utica, NE. "Cal was a fabulous fellow, loved by all, honest and true blue," Jan said. "He said he would happily take a horse back if it didn't work for Ponca. He said the horses we returned would be healthier, fatter, better feet and better trained." It was a time when truck-loads of horses from the Midwest would go regularly to New Holland, PA horse auctions."

Figure 10. The Mactiers bought Christopher Robin, "The Big Pride," as a three-year-old for $350. Pictured here at their home on North Post Road.

Mactier acquired some great horses from Cal Miller, but probably the greatest was The Big Pride/ Christopher Robin. Cal paid $25 to hide Pride from another horse dealer. Jan said, "Lucky us. The price was $350. He and Alibi Bart came at the same time. Pride was a very cheerful and exuberant horse." He always bucked but Jan learned to manage his antics to her advantage and the two hit it off. Christopher Robin took Jan through both B and A level testing in Pony Club and was loaned to the USET Olympic team in 1972.

Other horses were acquired from the area. Dr. Dutch Blose gave Ponca his retired Standardbred trotter Sweet Pea (renamed Powerhouse.) Everyone learned to post the trot on that horse, Jan laughed.

Figure 11. William Steinkraus riding Christopher Robin, "Pride," in training for the 1972 Olympic Games.

Ann established an annual summer camp for youngsters which continues today, over a half century later. Usually "sold out" well in advance, each camp includes a dozen or more youngsters who learn how to groom and ride horses. There are two sessions, each meeting three times a week for three weeks in early summer. On the final day there is a horse show, picnic, ribbons and T-shirts.

Sally and Corey Gaucasana came from Pioneer Park in Lincoln as instructors and to manage Ponca's barn. The summer camps were initially taught by Sally (later Sally Queal), who taught at Ponca for many years and remained close to Ponca Farm even after opening her own barn, "The Riding Center," across the street in the 90s.

Mike Blose, attended Ponca's first two Summer camps beginning at age 8. The Blose family had four horses on an acreage located in the hunt's Yorkshire country and Mike grew up riding and caring for them. Mike would hack his dad's big mounts over to Ponca to participate. The road was gravel and Mike remembers riding by the chicken farmer's house (now Jan and Mick Moriarty's house) and the hog farmer's house (now the Queals' Riding Center)

Figure 12. Jan Mactier riding "Pride" in a Farmington CT. show. He took her to Pony Club A rating.

Warren Weiner, Beth Maenner and Nina and Tammy Cudahy were also among the first campers. At the end of summer camp, the kids participated in a horse show. Nina Cudahy started riding at Ponca in 1966 at six years old. Blose remembers an early show where a camper was riding a big black off the track thoroughbred, Brother Joff. When the group was asked to canter, his horse thought he was back at the track and took off at a full gallop. He did multiple did laps around the arena before Dad (Dutch Blose) and Allan Mactier jumped in to stop him." Young rider Nancy Zandbergen, who also remembers Hireath, said, "Cory and Sally would allow me to have lessons on the famous Hiraeth, an Appaloosa that the Weiner family eventually bought. Now that was a great horse. Could do anything---Hunters-Jumpers-Pony Club. They don't make horses like him anymore!"

Hireath can be seen in many photos of the hunt and Pony Club rally teams. He came to Ponca as a chestnut gelding named Charlie's Snowflake. Sally Gaucasana named him Hireath, Welsh for 'Missing Home.' He had four white socks and was a registered Appaloosa. As time passed, he slowly became grey, then whiter and whiter, always with a flimsy mane and tail, Jan Moriarty explained. "Many people would remember Hireath. Few people would remember him as a chestnut."

Figure 13. Ponca Hills Indoor arena attracted a number of new riders who supplied the new hunt with members. Pictured from left, Susie Blackwell, Deb McKinnon on Hireath; Sally Gaucesana (Later Queal) and Gretchen Hennecke on Alibi Bart.

As the kids aged out of summer camp, they became camp assistants, helping teach the next youngsters. Several of Ponca's later instructors started at summer camp. Ponca's varied country, with its steep hills, flat valleys, challenging ravines, and cross-country jumps helped them develop into skilled riders. The experiences with this type of outdoor riding develop a firm seat which gave these kids an advantage in the arena, on jumping courses and in the hunt field.

Ponca Hills Farm became a Mecca for horse people. It was not only a place to learn but would become a center for equestrian families in the Midwest. Dick Hudson from Lincoln, who owned the Pepsi-Cola distributorship in Nebraska, came to Omaha to walk the land Allan bought for the barn. The Wofford family, then from the Fort Riley, KS, area, were early supporters, as were the John Grasmick family from Seward, NE, and the Lowell Boomer, the Burnham Yates and the Dwight Cherry families from Lincoln.

Eleanore MacDonald, who started riding at Ponca in 1965, recalls one day taking her horse Bliss (against Ann Mactier's very strict orders) on a long lovely hack to her grandparents' farm in Fort Calhoun. They traveled through the back roads, "through town and past enormous, loud, banging equipment working on the new freeway (Highway 75). Bliss was a gem, galloping the farm fields (after countless runaways at Ponca). Such a joy when one day we found a calm canter. Oh boy, did Ann give me hell, but it was sure worth it then." MacDonald also recalls her first show, "Up at 3 a.m. to braid and haul, hanging with the 'big kids,' as well as a few drag hunts and over smaller fences. Ponca, the people, the horses, all saved me as a young teen. Ann Mactier had a great deal to do with that, her kindness, her generosity, and her belief in me and what I could accomplish, are what I will never forget about her. Tough, strict, brilliant… yet compassionate. I think she knew that giving me Bliss to work (though heartbreaking in the end) would be just the medicine I needed. She was a great teacher of so many things for me." Eleanore came for the summers, staying with her grandparents. She still has a horse at her home in California.

In a May 6, 1968 letter to her children, Ann Mactier wrote about attending a show at Hillside Stables: "Bill Sol took about nine horses for us and Kay and her boyfriend took five in our truck. Tom won it on Rafe but fell off in the open. Poor Johnny Grasmick, who was so great on Lowell's pony can't do anything with his new mare. While his sister Amy, a year younger, is cleaning up on June Augie, Mary Yates' horse. Needless to say, Johnny's dad is tearing him apart. His mare is really balky, the daughter of Syncopate and one of Johnny's Hungarian thoroughbreds. Patti Miller looked nice on Becky and Tammy did fine on Happiness Is. Coco tossed Lisa Giltner and sent her to the hospital overnight for observation. Lisa and Tammy were riding double at the time."

A week later, Ann wrote, "Lisa had a spleen and kidney removed. And that will be the end of riding for that family. And the Cudahys must reconsider also. But Tina now says that Tammy will continue to ride. But Cocoa was Nina's pony and Cocoa has now wiped out Tracy Hardin twice and run away with Mary Mathews, and Happiness Is has broken Nancy Zandbergen's arm. Woe is everyone."

Mike Blose recalls that Ponca was heavily involved in horse shows in its early days. "I think there was an 'A rated' show at Ponca at least once a year." Nina Cudahy boarded and rode her horse at Ponca from 1969 to 1981. Sally continued to teach the youngest riders while more advanced riders were instructed by a variety of excellent instructors. Alex Adams, Gretchen Hennecke, Sue Martin, Deb McKinnon, Tom Ordway and Rich Eckhardt all were instructors during Ponca Hills Farm's first decade. Ordway came to Ponca New Year's Day, 1969 where he met Debbie McKinnon at the Mactier home. He left for France in 1972 but came back to manage Ponca in 1976. Eckhardt was also Ponca manager and trainer.

Keeping many horses healthy was a continuing challenge and Jan Moriarty remembers some of Ponca's early veterinarians Dr. Lewis and ex-Cavalryman, Dr. Ben Moore. "Dr. Moore was a special guy. He was always well-dressed. He wore a dark suit coat, white shirt, tie or bolero. He was not young. We figured out there weren't any vet schools around when he would have gone to school. He was great at lameness but not so great at internal problems.

"He was known to swear like a sailor, but not if a lady was present. Occasionally he would apologize to my mom for a verbal slip," Jan said. "He was a great racetrack vet. A constant prescription was 'Aw hell. There ain't nothing wrong with that horse. Just ride 'em.' When Pride went to Olympic Team headquarters in New Jersey we had news that he was lame. Ben Moore called Bert de Nemethy, a Hungarian Cavalry Officer who coached the Olympic Jumping team and talked to him about the horse. Moore said, 'Hell. There ain't anything wrong. Just ride him.' They did and all was well."

Moore had various liniments and homemade remedies, blisters, pin-firing that worked well. Air bubbles put by bulb and tube in between the skin and muscle smoothed around by hand and then White's Liniment applied topically for "Sweeney Shoulder."

Dr. Burton Smith, younger than Dr. Lewis, started coming to Ponca and gradually did more and more work. Ponca was glad to have a second vet available. Later came a young Dr. Lowell Smalley, who was Ponca's main vet until he retired. Dr. Bernie Fletcher, Dr. Hutchinson, and Dr. Brunk were regulars at Ponca. Smalley's Nebraska Equine Vet Clinic, today headed by Dr. Mike Black, continues to treat horses at Ponca.

The Hunt Expands, Spurred by Friends, and Junior Riders.

Figure 14. Pony Clubbers contribute many junior riders to the hunt. Pictured is the Pony Club Team- all fox hunters in the early days of the hunt. From left: Sharon Naughton, Kathy Armstrong, Beth Maenner, and Jon Ketzler with Beth Novak (front).

Invitations to join the North Hills Hunt were hand-written for a number of years. The initial roster in 1966 showed the Hunt had 19 members. MFH Taylor Snow was designated huntsman, Dr. Irvin (Dutch) Blose and Charles Nelson were whippers-in, and Donovan Ketzler was selected field master. Original members also included James Adams, Dr. Charles Bonniwell, Don Dunn, Corey Gacusana, Fred Nance, and Arthur Pinkerton.

North Hills' members worked hard getting riders from Lincoln involved from its first days. In 1966 Lincoln members included Dr. Dwight Cherry (who owned the famous jumper Cherry Coke) and his son John, Dick and Ann Hudson, and Lowell Boomer, who founded, headed and paid the expenses of the United States Dressage Federation for years. Other non-Omahans who joined the Hunt in 1966 included Mrs. Eloise Joyce, Mr. and Mrs. Frank Roehl, Mr. and Mrs. Burnham Yates from Lincoln, and Dr. and Mrs. Paul Mooring from Fort Calhoun. Moorings had an acreage and, for many years, hosted the Hunt's "Day in the Country."

John and Jewel Grasmick came from Seward to hunt. John transported his horse in the bed of a pickup truck with the horse's head tied to the cab. When he arrived, Grasmick turned the horse around in the pickup bed and the horse jumped out. To load him at the end of the hunt, he backed the pickup truck up to a small hill and the horse jumped in. He re-tied him to the cab and drove back to Seward. Grasmick's son, Johnny Grasmick, was an active jockey, racing Thoroughbreds. He started hunting in the very early days of the Hunt with Amy, his sister, and later was awarded his buttons. He had a pickup and a two-horse trailer so he could take three horses…one in the back of the pickup. John Grasmick had a Hungarian Thoroughbred, aptly called Big Enough. Jewel recalls there "was a time or two when I think he accidentally rode ahead of the Master".

The Grasmick family also had success with their show mare, June Augie, and John later stood the famous Thoroughbred stallion, Hurry to Market, at his farm. John was a colorful fellow with a droll wit who was known for speaking his mind. He had a particular dislike for ponies, and once was heard saying "we should just spray for them." After John was awarded his colors, he quit hunting because, it is told, he flat out refused to invest in a red coat. Not surprising, since he also refused to wear a tux at his daughter's wedding!

Lowell Boomer remembered the time Dr. Ackerman from Lincoln found a fox kit whose mother was killed. He called Lowell suggesting he take it to the Hunt. Lowell put it in a box and drove it to Omaha, intending to give to Taylor Snow. But Snow didn't want it at his factory and told him to take it to Ketzler's garage. Bette Ketzler, not appreciating the smell, had a fit. So Ketzler, Snow and some others took it out to the country thinking they could let the hounds smell real fox. When they got to the hunt country with the kit fox and a few hounds, kinder, gentler heads prevailed, and they let the kit run into the woods without the hounds.

By 1967, North Hills Hunt's roster listed 27 families. New members included Norman Bengston, (who later became Master of Foxhounds) Mr. and Mrs. Philip Giltner, and Harry Koch. The 1967-68 season roster also added Sebastian Caniglia, Anthony Cudahy, Philip Dubrow, Dennis Gilstad, Freeman "Bud" Godfrey, George Matthews, Carl Renstrom, Robert Wahl, and H.D. Zandbergen. Many of these families had children who were riding.

Figure 15. Serious work, and fun with horses has led to lifelong friendships which began at Ponca Hills Farm. From left, Marin Mitchell, Rob Mactier, Gretchen Hennecke, Tom Ordway, Tammy Cudahy, Charlie Zaayer, Jan Mactier, Lisa Giltner, Deb McKinnon, and Pooh (Ordway's Bull Terrier from England.)

In its early years, many riders who boarded horses at Ponca Hills Farm were able to hack to different fixtures in the area. These included Yorkshire and Tanglewood, which ran east of 60th street and west of Highway 75 from McKinley Road (Highway 36) to Northern Hills Drive; the north and south Stratbucker countries, west on

Highway 75 and north to Fort Calhoun; And the Duda River Run, neighboring country east of Ponca Hills Farm on the east side of River Road intersecting with Ponca Road.

Children of the Hunt founders, most members of Pony Club, and their friends who rode at Ponca, joined in the fun. They included Jan Mactier, Mike Blose, Donovan Ketzler's sons Jon and Jeff, and Nancy Duhnke's son John. Mike Blose remembers that he spent all his time fox hunting, which he preferred to horse showing. His family later bought 20 acres closer to Ponca.

Youth participation was always encouraged and NHH was the hunt with the largest number of junior riders on staff in the country. During the early 70s, the Hunt was frequently riding out from Ponca Hills Farm where many of the junior riders had horses, and so the Hunt continued to be strengthened by the addition of more competent junior riders including Blair Cudmore, Brian Bengston, Dee Hudson, Stacy Truesdell, Stacy "Stretch" Godfrey, Valerie Grauer, Nina and Tami Cudahy, Diane Leaders, Bob Wagner, Rob Mactier, Tom Caniglia, Mary Dunham, Jean Mergens, Patti Miller, Busy Schenken, Kay Blose and Kim Bonniwell.

Dick and Ann Hudson's daughter, Dee, recalls, "When I was 12 years old, I fox hunted at Ponca. In the early morning, they would drag a scent, which made for a very fun ride. I hunted a few times at Ponca alongside the Cudmore boys, Mike Blose, Brian Bengston, Jon Ketzler, Jeff Ketzler, Jim Urban, Lindsey Stratbucker, Brent, Brian, and Blair Cudmore just to name a few. Dutch Blose was our Master at that time, followed by Van Ketzler. I also remember whippers-in Don Dunn, Jim Sophir, and Larry Stratman. Bob Stubblefield, Sherma and Lyle Seitzinger, Allan Mactier, and my parents, were faces that I saw frequently in the field."

"Afterwards, we youngsters would have so much fun together. While our parents were socializing, we would too. We would go up onto Phil's Hill and look out over Omaha. I remember many fun times, and a lot of great laughs on that hill. It bonded us all together, along with our love for horses."

Mike Blose recalls being frequently grounded by his father because of bad grades which began to slip as he discovered girls and fox hunting. "I started hunting in about sixth or seventh grade....my old man let me go out a few times. We used to start out fox hunting at Ponca, then at Stratbucker's near Ft. Calhoun. We also hunted Tanglewood." When Blose was in high school he was a whipper-in with Jon Ketzler, Jim Urban, and Brian Bengston. "It kept me out of trouble," he says.

Blose explained: "I was used to big horses because Allan and dad had big horses for hunting. One was Powerhouse and another was Friar Tuck. Friar Tuck was so big that you couldn't get into the straight stall to groom him. I went around and put hay in the manger and stood on that to brush him."

One memorable first hunt for a junior rider evolved into family lifetime memories for six riding members. Karman Seitzinger DeLuca loved the show ring but really wanted to go fox hunting. Her parents, Lyle and Sherma Seitzinger, were concerned this sport had a reputation for wild drinking and unsafe riding but were finally convinced to let their 14-year-old daughter to go out on one of the hunts. She and her horse Schatze would get along fine with Jack Eden as her safety net. She and Derry Seldin met Jack at Ponca Hills Farm. Karman convinced her parents to get involved with horses and join the Hunt. Her brother Jayson and sister Kristal also became active in hunting and also served as whips.

Jan Mactier rode with the Hunt when she was home from boarding school. She remembered, "They would ask me to go hunting, and I would say 'Only if you make sure the horse you give me has hunted before.' Of course, they gave me one that had never hunted and was wild and an exciting ride."

Jim Urban had his horse at Ponca. Rumor has it that he was primarily attracted to the Hunt because of all the girls in tight pants, a rumor he doesn't deny. H.D. Zandbergen and Al Grauer both worked for the phone company and hunted. Grauer's wife, Julie was a NHH whip and their son and daughter both rode at Ponca.

The adult members were great mentors for the junior riders. Don Dunn saw to things that needed to be done and got them done and was a great mediator. An early boarder at Ponca Hills, he always volunteered to help the kids with their homework, especially chemistry, since he ran the lab at a local hospital. Jan Moriarty remembers: "Dunn was always so kind and you couldn't ever ruffle him. There were shenanigans going on with the kids, but Mr. Dunn would never turn you in. Don was there every day… always available for homework. Don Dunn was also a Deacon. For years he blessed the hounds at opening hunts and participated in some of the Hunt marriages, including that of Jack and Robyn Carmichael."

"Van Ketzler followed the cavalry manual on horse care and riding," Jan Moriarty remembers. "If something wasn't working with horses, we always had the cavalry manual to tell us the right way. Ketzler also conducted drill team exercises with the kids. But we never had to ride in McClellan Saddles because Van agreed they were not that comfortable."

Pony Clubber Nancy Zandbergen fondly remembers "the hunting we all did from Ponca as juniors, the folks that boarded at Ponca and more. Just a super memory all the way around."

"A Day in the Country" was established in 1976 as a Hunt tradition with the first event held at Ponca Hills Farm. This was a day-long event with cross-country and arena classes for riders and a picnic for riders and spectators. That fall the Hunter Pace was held at Dr. Paul Mooring's farm in Ft. Calhoun. Ponca Farm was the setting for Opening Hunt, where 136 people were served breakfast after the hunt.

The North Hills Hunt Show was discussed at a meeting on September 30, 1979 and it was decided that it should become an annual event every May and that it should be registered and rated with the American Horse Show Association (AHSA). NHH held a May horse show almost every year usually on the Memorial Day weekend. Early venues were Ponca Hills Farm, Arlington Fairgrounds and Glencarry Stable in Crescent, Iowa.

Allan Mactier – Master of Foxhounds

Busy as CEO of Nebraska Consolidated Mills, a major corporation, Allan Mactier, always a force in the Hunt, spent his weekends fox hunting whenever he was in town. A tall man on a tall horse, always impeccably turned out, Allan cut a dashing figure in his top hat. With his droll wit and winning smile, he was the soul of graciousness, making everyone from hill toppers to first flight, car followers and landowners feel they were important members of the hunting tradition. He was named Master of Foxhounds in 1980.

Allan had an amazing ability to turn even moments of imminent disaster into social occasions. On one occasion, while galloping up a narrow, wooded trail, Allan encountered a low hanging branch. The unlikely result was that he fell "up" the tree. Though unseated from his horse, he clung to the branch and amiably doffed his bowler hat to the riders who had followed and were galloping on by him.

One thing early riders learned when riding in the field with Allan: it was not always a good idea to follow him. Though he looked the part of a commanding leader, he was given, on occasion, to take his own line, not necessarily that of the hounds. Whether this was due to his natural curiosity, his adventurous spirit or perhaps a faulty sense of direction, his fellow fox hunters were never sure. Daughter Jan remembers, "You could be with him and end up God knows where, with the sun going down and the wind blowing cold and barbed wire fences blocking the way back."

Allan had a life-long love of fox hunting and eagerly sought opportunities to ride with different Hunts throughout the United States and particularly Ireland. It was a love he shared with his son-in-law, Mick Moriarty, throughout his life.

Over the years, Ponca Farm hosted a number of foxhunting luminaries, including Matthew Mackay-Smith, publishing editor of the prestigious Chronicle of the Horse; the renowned Thady Ryan, Master of Ireland's Scarteen Black & Tans; and legendary American fox hunter Ben Hardaway from Georgia.

The North Hills Hunt which Allan Mactier helped to start, owes much of its early vitality to the barn he built and the traditions he established. Today it is flourishing with a field of young riders from Iowa and Nebraska. It has weathered many crises, had English, Irish and home-grown huntsmen, has permanent kennels, huntsman's house and clubhouse near Loveland, Iowa, and hunts regularly in several venues in both Iowa and Nebraska. It has become known for its invitational hunt in Burwell, NE, where its spring and fall hunts draw riders from many states as well as a contingent of local riders.

Ponca Pony Club

While Allan was involved with the early years of the North Hills Hunt, Ann, who had finished her second degree, a Bachelor of Arts, (University of Nebraska at Omaha, 1963), saw an important role for the new barn in educating young riders. A method to accomplish that was discovered when Philip Durbrow, young bootstrapper at UNO, appeared at Ponca wanting to get involved. Durbrow saw a newspaper article about the opening of Nebraska's first fox hunt and called Taylor Snow. Snow suggested he talk to Allan Mactier who might give him a job.

Durbrow had worked for Richard "Dick" Collins, at the Pebble Beach Equestrian Center in California as a stable hand and rider, who also designed their 1969 National Three-Day Event course. The Pebble Beach Center was home to the Olympic Three-Day Team and for several years Collins was the coach. Collins and his wife Marguarite who were like parents to Phil, were committed to the education of young equestrians. They started the first United States Pony Club chapter on the West Coast in 1954. He also ran successful summer camps and hunter trials on the West Coast. Durbrow introduced the Mactiers to Collins. The couples became friends, with Allan and Ann, frequently visiting the Pebble Beach center and fox hunting with them in Ireland. Through Collins, Ann learned that Pony Club was an organization with similar goals to hers. She started the first United States Pony Club chapter in Nebraska, Ponca Pony Club, which has trained hundreds of young riders for over 50 years.

Pony Clubs in the United States were an offshoot of the British Pony Clubs that had been going since 1929 as a branch of the Institute of the Horse. The USPC founders were enthusiastic fox hunters who recognized the need for an organization to provide sound instruction for all interested children, especially those who otherwise could not afford expensive lessons.

A new Pony Club, if it is located in territory of a hunt registered by the Masters of Foxhounds Association, needs approval from that hunt. Master of Fox Hounds of North Hills Hunt, Taylor Snow, knew about Pony Clubs and saw them as an excellent way to train young riders to future members of the Hunt. The new club had a strong base of support. Ponca Hills Pony Club had already recruited members and was having mounted meetings by the time it was officially established June 7, 1967.

In a letter sent April 30, 1967 approving Ponca Pony Club as an affiliate of USPC, Roberta Folonie, Midwest Supervisor, wrote:

"The Ponca Hills Pony Club appears to be a well-organized group which has been established for some time. The opportunity for leadership among parents is strong. The relationship with the existing foxhunt is close. Taylor Snow, M.F.H., wholeheartedly endorses the Pony Club, and is personally helping with instruction.

The existing physical facilities, both indoors and outdoors, are excellent. The Ponca Hills Riding Academy is located within the fox hunting territory. The opportunity for equitation and general horsemanship is above average.

In answer to your question concerning amateur/professional, Anne (sic) Mactier is definitely not a professional. The Ponca Hills Pony Club is fortunate to have Mrs. Mactier as District Commissioner. She has a lifetime of experience in horsemanship. She is a woman of diversified interests; she is currently finishing work toward a master's degree in English, while teaching at a high school in a deprived area. She in no way derives any income from her horse activities.

I wish to recommend that the Ponca Hills Pony Club be added to the list of members of the United States Pony Clubs, Inc."

Ann served as leader of the new club for a year before it was chartered, then officially as District Commissioner (DC) from 1967 until 1970. She continued as Joint DC for three years in the 70s. The position of DC is a tremendous undertaking and involves record keeping, planning of mounted and horsemanship knowledge lessons and testing, keeping the young riders challenged and securing mounts for those who do not have their own horses, arranging for riding instructors and facilities, and coordinating trips to regional "Know Downs" and mounted rallies.

The Articles of Organization list Ponca Pony Club's territory as "Omaha and Lincoln, Nebraska." The Cornhusker Pony Club, with territories of Lancaster and Seward Counties, was officially established by the USPC nationally on May 20, 1967, one month later, at Possum's Hollow. Cornhusker Pony Club's original DCs were Lowell Boomer and John Grasmick. (Grasmick's had horses at their place on Old Cheney Road and later in Seward.) Lowell and his son, John, as well as Burnham and Mary Yates were the original sponsors of Cornhusker Pony Club. The originating barn was Pioneer Stables at Pioneer Park, Lincoln. At that time, the Ponca club was by far the most active and had a large membership and supportive parents. Ponca and Cornhusker Pony Clubs were established just one month apart and largely by members of the North Hills Hunt and the group of riding friends of Allan and Ann Mactier.

Pony Clubs emphasize horsemanship, not just riding ability. Members learn how to care for their horses, including health care and first aid, nutrition, stable management, tack and how to ride safely, correctly and confidently. Pony Clubbers also learn respect for their horses, themselves, the land and the importance of conservation. Service and a sense of volunteerism is encouraged. Members progress through ranks at their own individual pace, achieving personal goals through expanded knowledge and experience.

Riders are organized into teams for competitions, where they learn the value of cooperation, communication, responsibility, mentoring, teaching and fostering supportive relationships – experience that builds leadership skills. Teams compete in rallies at the regional level, where they may also qualify to compete in national rallies. Rallies consist of written tests, stable management inspections, and riders who compete in dressage, cross-country and show jumping. Today Pony Club has competitions in Eventing, Games, Polo Crosse, Tetrathlon, Polo, and Quiz (non-riding, knowledge based).

Initially, riders work to become a D1 and then D2 and are tested on safety around horses, knowledge about horses and horse care as well as mounted riding tests. As they progress through C level, both the horse management tests and the riding tests become more detailed and more challenging. Testing at all levels is done by experienced Pony Club graduates and at C level, the test might take two days.

When a rider tests for B rating, tests are conducted by experienced professional including veterinarians. It should be noted that only a dedicated few riders achieve B and A ratings and those who do are recognized worldwide as an experienced rider and horse professional. They are capable of training and testing others and of operating a working horse stable.

Ponca Group Jumps into Competition

Figure 16. Ponca Pony Club's first team (1967) Pictured at Kansas City Rally, from left, Deb McKinnon, Jan Mactier, Kim Bonniwell, Gretchen Hennecke and Beth Novak.

Ponca Pony Club started by jumping right into regional competition. Its few members had not yet started to study and practice the strict Pony Club guidelines when Ann Mactier learned about a regional Pony Club Rally being held in Kansas City in 1967 and thought they should go.

She asked her daughter Jan, home from boarding school, to be captain of the C Pony Club team, to which Jan asked, "What is Pony Club?" Ann put together a team that included good riders who were game for the challenge. Kim Bonniwell was stable manager. Gretchen Hennecke, Deb McKinnon, Jan Mactier, and Beth Novak filled out the team. Jan and Debbie bought T Shirts for the team.

The team held their own considering it was their first exposure to the highly regulated Pony Club competition. They learned that judging at these rallies was as much on horse care, horsemanship, and teamwork as on riding ability and placing in events.

• JUL • **67**

Figure 17. Dressed in Overalls They were coached by Phil Durbrow, 1967.

Jan remembers Gretchen Henneke in a competition yelled "God Damn You" to her horse and the team was penalized 15 points. The team lost but did not come in last and so the first Ponca Pony Club team to enter competition was deemed a success!

Other teenage riders at Ponca made up that first club. Going up through the levels of Pony Club, these Ponca kids became competent riders and began showing and fox hunting with the North Hills Hunt. At Ponca, kids learned the basics at the summer camps then moved right into Pony Club. For example, Mike Blose, in the first summer camp at age 8, began riding and competing with the Pony Club by age 12. Ponca Pony Club members were first introduced to fox hunts by invitation to their whole group.

North Hills Hunt scheduled Junior hunts and as the junior riders' abilities increased, several junior members became staff whips. Pony Club riders participating in hunts often hacked to the hunt venue from Ponca Hills Farm. By riding outside over rough terrain, jumping coops and ditches, riders developed a secure seat which helped them master indoor and outdoor riding tests in Pony Club ratings and served them well when competing in horse shows and events. Throughout the years of Pony Club and of the North Hills Hunt, Pony Clubbers have turned out for hunts and hunt activities.

Ann Mactier in a 1968 letter to her children, wrote: "I really like Pony Club. It is organized and hard and demanding and teaches one a lot, especially how little they know. Pony Club helps you to know that there is a lot you don't know about this kind of riding and how to go about learning it."

Charter members of Ponca Pony Club in 1968 included: Stacy Adams, Sharon, Katharine and Susan Armstrong, Brian Bengston, Susan Blackwell, Kay and Mike Blose, Kim Bonniwell, Tom Caniglia, Mary Cannon, Jeanne Clure, Kiki Crummer, Nina, Hope and Tammy Cudahy, John and Todd Duhnke, Jan Elston, Sally Gaines, Dennis Gilstad, Lisa Giltner, Stacy Godfrey, Tracy Harding, Chuck Harris, Mary Jo Harrison, Gretchen Hennecke, Jon Ketzler, Tessie Levers, Jan and Rob Mactier, Beth Maenner, Mary Matthews, Mimi Marcotte, Debbie McKinnon, Patti Melcher, Jean Mergens, Mindy Nance, Patti and Susan Miller, Beth Novak, Terri Lynn Parker, John Pilcher, Lisa Renstrom, Kirsten Robinson, Karen Schleiger, Leslie Tamisea, Patty Tewhill, Stacy Truesdell, Mari and Mark Wahl, Pat Watson, Warren Weiner, and Nancy Zandbergen. Jan Mactier and Debbie McKinnon both had their B rating from USPC before Ponca Pony Club was officially recognized by USPC.

Kids Learn from Experts, Supported by Parents

Figure 18. **Phil Durbrow,** a "boot strapper" at UNO became a Ponca fixture. He introduced the Mactiers to Dick Collins, who introduced them to fox hunting in Ireland and to Pony Club as a way to train young riders.

In its January 1968 report to USPC, Ponca's club said they had helped in building a cross-country course, held a rally, and held clinics on fox hunting and cross-country riding. They also fielded two C teams for the Regional Rally, an effort enhanced by the enthusiastic participation of Phil Durbrow, who spent hours at Ponca coaching the teams and building fences. The report to USPC said, "The Lord provided one ex-pony clubber, Phil Durbrow who had ten days to train the teams." Phil volunteered to train the teams for an upcoming rally. "I remember preparing the team for going East by running around the property on foot and saying, 'jump this, jump that.' Picket fence, in and out, fallen logs, ditches, all things that were not jumps, but were in some cases pretty challenging. Because they were following each other, they never backed off and got the confidence that they could jump anything," Durbrow said.

"I remember when the Raccoon Valley pony club "B" team went back east for the Nationals, they all dressed in farmer's overalls around the barns, because they knew that's how the Easterners thought of them, and they just wanted to have fun with it," Durbrow said. "Then they won the B nationals, and all the Easterners had to come to Iowa, which they thought was the end of the world. Later they came to Nebraska for the 1973 National finals, and surprise! They found Nebraska beautiful and the people friendly and capable."

"The kids in the Pony Club were all different individuals, with different backgrounds, and horses of different capabilities, but they really came together as a team and supported each other. They were a very nice group of kids," Durbrow said.

Jan Mactier won the B Regional Rally in Des Moines as an Individual and then won as a three-man Team with Debbie McKinnon and Gretchen Hennecke. A three-man team can't qualify for Nationals. Ponca had only 3 Bs so Jan qualified for a spot on a regional B Team. That Team went to National Rally in Myopia, MA 1970. It was exciting and Jan remembers: "We left from Wayne Du Page, Illinois using their equipment and colors. The Rally was at Neil Ayer's and the Myopia Hunt Club, at Hamilton, MA. Everyone said the sun rises and sets over Neil Ayer. He designed Three-Day Cross-country courses for national competitions including rallies, and the Los Angeles Olympics. He later came to the National Pony Club Rally in Omaha in 1973."

"Mom and I drove April Dancer "Becky," Mom's horse, to Wayne DuPage joining the other team members and horses. Then they shipped by commercial carrier to Myopia. It is 1900 miles from Omaha to Myopia," Jan said.

The event included a number of people who later came to Ponca, according to Jan. "I now know that my dear friends Joy Slater, as a B, and Tom Ordway as an A were competing there. We had not met yet. I think Tom's B Team from Glastonbury, Connecticut won the Rally. I think Ann Shepherd, a later Ponca instructor. was there too. Rick Eckhardt was from Glastonbury Pony Club."

Packing horses, tack, feed and equipment is a major undertaking and Pony Clubbers are schooled in making checklists for the trip because anything forgotten can be a disaster. On this trip, Jan said, "I forgot to pack my breeches. This was a major problem because they had to be custom made. At that time 2/4 way stretch fabric and long leg patterns did not exist so I could not buy breeches off the rack. There were no English, Hunt Seat, tack stores in Nebraska. Miller Harness mail order catalog was the source of all equipment. My measurements were sent to purchase breeches. They replied 'remeasure. Your measurements are wrong.' The measurements were correct." Jan was very tall and very thin with very long legs!

"No pants was a big problem. Mom called Dad. As instructed, Dad went to my closet and found my breeches on their hanger. He took them to the office and handed them to his secretary Francis Schuster. She went to the airport and talked to the United stewardesses. 'Could they possibly help?' In Chicago the breeches, on their hanger, were handed to the stewardess on the flight to Boston. When the plane arrived in Boston, mom was waiting at the gate. I received my breeches on their hanger just in time. At that time there was no speed mail, Fed Ex or UPS."

Ponca Pony Club parents played a major role in getting the extensive study materials out to over 40 kids and helping them study subjects they themselves didn't know. They raised money for the rally team's travel expenses and testing. The January 1969 year-end report to USPC said: "In May, a competitive trail ride raised no funds, but the beef was good." The next year Ponca qualified one B rider. In June, three C's and three B's and six horses competed in a regional rally 700 miles away. The C's took third place.

Ann Mactier wrote in a letter to her children: "I'm getting as bad as Phil, a perfectionist. That is, I don't like to see people just pushing horses around. I would rather see a really beautiful ride than a flashy jumper. Dad and Phil have been laying out a ten to fifteen-mile trail ride for our benefit to raise money for Pony Club. Phil is so appreciative of nature that one gets a lift just being with him."

Nancy Zandbergen Wilson remembers: "Ann Mactier wrote me a memorable/short note when I was going for my B in Pony Club, right after I returned from camp in North Carolina. (I went every summer and missed being at Ponca.) Ann's words were tough but straight from our dedicated DC. She said, 'B testing is no fooling around, Nancy. Better get to work and study hard.' I have that note ingrained in my brain and will never forget it. Thank goodness I was successful and received my B on a borrowed horse at the Raccoon Valley Pony Club, Des Moines testing. I was one of the youngest in the country to get it that year and thankfully did not fail. I was scared to death of Ann!" Nancy was only 15 in 1969!

Ann Mactier was determined that riders were educated by the best instructors they could bring to Omaha. For years, nationally and internationally known clinicians such as George Morris, Karl Mikolka, Jan Conant, Gordon Wright, Bengt Ljungquist, Gabor Foltenyi, Hans Senn, and others came regularly to teach.

Lowell Boomer, DC of Cornhusker Pony Club, frequently came to Omaha to participate in Ponca Pony Club instruction as well as fox hunting. He held meetings and mounted lessons at his barn in Lincoln. A founder of the United Stated Dressage Association, Boomer was its president for many years, provided much of its funding, and established its headquarters in Lincoln.

Club Members Compete Regionally, Nationally

In January 1970, Ponca reported a membership of 68 (56 girls and 12 boys). They had 4 B's (Jan Mactier, Gretchen Hennecke, Debbie McKinnon, and Nancy Zandbergen) and 15 C's. (Jim Urban joined the group that year as a 12-year-old.) That year the group held a rally, had bake sales and a raffle of Dehner Boots to raise money. The annual report noted: "The youngsters are beginning to realize that Pony Club is a labor of love by many people from which they, the members, reap the benefit, and therefore the debt also, an obligation to be givers, not just takers, of Pony Club. We are all proud of Ponca, now in its third year, and proud of the contributions it has made to a fine sport which rewards hard work, cooperation, self-discipline with health and obvious accomplishments, and also with less obvious good feelings of harmony in nature, animals, people, and oneself."

The Club continued to grow as did the group of supportive parents, in 1971. Some non-riding parents decided to learn to ride, some helped build jumps and organized lessons, and others supplied refreshments and transportation for the kids. Jan Mactier, the club's only A, competed in the National Rally in Bath, OH. Jon Ketzler and Jean Mergens achieved B ratings. Ponca hosted a D level rally as a way to give beginning riders more experience. Kenneth Naughton joined Don Dunn as Joint DC. Naughton, father of Club member Sharon Naughton, served as DC for nine years, until 1980.

By this time, Ponca Pony Club had hosted a number of rallies at Ponca Hills Farm, including a Regional Rally. It sent two C level teams and two B level teams to the Regional Rally in Des Moines where Ponca's C team took third place. John Ruan, founder of a major trucking company, was an important sponsor of the Des Moines Raccoon Valley Pony Club. The Des Moines group drove to a National Pony Club Rally in Fairfield, CT, hauling all the horses in a long stock trailer. That method of transport shocked the Easterners, but the team took first place. Both Des Moines and Ponca were getting positive recognition by the United States Pony Club for their active clubs. Together the parents of the two groups discussed the possibility of bringing a National Pony Club Rally to Ponca Hills Farm. Allan Mactier stepped up to bid on the competition and Omaha was chosen. Ponca would host the National Rally in 1973.

In 1972, Glenn and Carole Cudmore moved to Omaha from Canada as managers and trainers at Ponca Hills Farm. They had four boys: Brent, the oldest, was 11. The boys all became members of Pony Club. That year, George Morris came at Christmas for a clinic and Gabor Foltanyi came at Thanksgiving to do a dressage clinic.

Labeled the Club's "most exciting year," 1972 was dominated by the anticipation of the National Rally. The Club added more activities and more members went through the rigorous studying and testing to achieve higher ratings. Debbie McKinnon joined Jan Mactier in achieving an A rating, and the C2 team took fourth at a regional rally. That year there were several Pony Club designated days for hunting with North Hills Hunt and the group also got an introduction to polo!

By 1973, Ponca Pony Club membership had grown to 64 (46 girls and 18 boys) with seven B rated members. New B rated members included: Patti Miller, Sharon Naughton, Jim Urban, and Warren Weiner. Naughton was just 14, the youngest B rated rider. Members John Steenburg, Warren Weiner and Mike Blose also worked cutting and baling hay at Ponca in the summer

U.S. Pony Club Holds National Rally at Ponca Hills Farm

The announcement that Ponca Hills Farm would be the site of the National Rally for the U.S. Pony Club July 25 - 29, 1973 set off a firestorm of activity. Jan Mactier Moriarty said, "No one knew what they were doing, but there were plenty of volunteers willing to learn." Many boarders and Hunt members stepped up to volunteer hundreds of hours for the rally.

Tony Cudahy headed the effort and was in charge of stadium jumping. Bud Godfrey and Robyn Carmichael were his assistants. Jack Eden took pictures. Offutt Air Force Base personnel volunteered to handle communications. Van Ketzler helped build the jumps. Ed Miller, Bud Godfrey, Daniel Mergens, Ken Naughton and John "Jack" Maenner all handled major volunteer roles.

Former USEF Eventing Chef d'Equipe, Jack LeGoff, coach of the United States Three-Day Olympic Team, designed the cross-country competition course, taking advantage of Ponca's steep hills, open meadows and woodlands. Ken Naughton helped build the individual cross-country jumps with Van Ketzler, Rob Mactier, and some of Rob's friends. Today many of LeGoff's original fences have been refurbished and the course continues to expand. Over 50 elements, including banks and water complexes, comprise three courses with options for beginners, novice, and preliminary levels.

Figure 19. Riders take the triple bar log jump on Ponca's cross-country course.

Ponca's cross-country course of approximately 2 ¾ to 4 miles, included up to 36 fixed, solid obstacles, designed to present varying degrees of challenges to horse and rider. Though built to look natural, some materials and decorations were made to test the horse and rider's bravery and ability to choose the best option for negotiating the fences. Jumps included a new horizon jump, a challenging sheep's pen, water hazard, Trakehner jump over ditches, the multi-step piano jump, triple bar logs and the "Phil's Hill" banks. Riders faced changes in lighting, optional lines, straightforward as well as corner option, and skinny jumps.

The volunteers had the honor of working with famous equestrian judges, including Olympians Bruce Davidson, J. Michael Plumb and Jimmy Wofford from the U.S. Three-Day Eventing Olympic Team, who donated their time. Thaddeus Ryan from Scarteen Hunt in Ireland came to Omaha to help judge. The Mactiers had fox hunted with the Scarteen in Ireland and Ryan was contracted by Allan Mactier to be the face of a new dog food produced by Nebraska Consolidated Mills.

Figure 20. Thaddeus Ryan from Scarteen Hunt in Ireland came to Omaha to help judge the National Pony Club Rally held at Ponca in 1973. Other judges included Olympians Bruce Davidson, J. Michael Plumb and Jimmy Wofford from the U.S. Three-Day Event.

Pat Rothe, a Ponca boarder who volunteered to help, remembers walking the cross-country course with Ann Mactier, who "could identify all the various grasses and bushes and their uses by early native inhabitants of the land." Rothe remembers competitors coming from the East were totally amazed by the hills.

Bette Ketzler, who helped with mailings and registration, remembered advance warnings to participants: "There are three Hs in Omaha: Heat, Humidity, and Hills." She said most visiting equestrians thought Nebraska was flat and didn't take the warning seriously. Taking care of overly hot horses, unconditioned for the steep hills of Ponca, became an important focus.

Figure 21. Judges stand as the national anthem kicks off the National Pony Club Rally on Ponca's Front Pasture July 29, 1973. Pictured from left to right, Jack Fritz, long time National Pony Club Chairman; Alice Reidy, USPC; Col. Howard C. Fair, President, National Pony Club; Allan Mactier; F. Philip Giltner, Ponca Pony Club; Owen Fleming, Raccoon Valley Pony Club; Ken Naughton, Ponca Pony Club; and Erskine Bedford, USPC and MFH Piedmont Hunt.

Merrilee Hansen, a boarder at Ponca, recalls observing at a cross-country jump on the course when a rider from Florida was dumped by a refusal. He leapt to his feet saying, "The flatlands of Nebraska - who would have thought there would be so many hills."

Club Continues to Educate Through Clinics, Competition in 70s

Figure 22. Teams competed at Maffitt Lake, Des Moines. From left, Vem Salestrom, D.C., Janet Lynch, Sandy Smalley, Cheryl Cook, Merrilee Hansen (parent), Kirstin Wagner, Hillary Horner and Kay Salestrom.

With all the activity in 1973, Ponca Pony Club saw its B team finish 2nd and its C1 and C2 teams finished 1st at a Regional Rally. The club welcomed 34 new members and ranked near the top of the nation with 18 male members!

Some of the kids participating in the early 70s included Kathy, Sharon and Susan Armstrong, Jan, Kay and Mike Blose, Tom Caniglia, Katie and Mary Cannon, Nina and Tammy Cudahy, Kathy Drahota, Jan and Shari Elston, Sally Gaines, Lisa Giltner, Stacy Godfrey, Christine, Mary Jo and Bill Harrison, Sally Jennings, Jon and Jeff Ketzler, Carol and Mimi Marcotte, Debbie McKinnon, Barb and Patti Melcher, Anne and Joan Mergans, Patti and Susanne Miller, Sharon Naughton, Jody

Newman, Mary Offutt, Lisa Renstrom, Martha Rigby, Elizabeth Schenken, Karen Schleger, Leslie Tamisiea, Patty Tewhill, Stacy Truesdell, Jim Urban, Mari Wahl, Pat Watson, Laura Weinberger, Warren Weiner, Mary Ann Wright and Nancy Zandbergen.

The Club's eight B Rated members by 1974 included Tammy Cudahy, Stacy Godfrey, Jon Ketzler, Pattie Miller, Sharon Naughton, Jim Urban, Nancy Zandbergen and Stephanie Noonan. The roster also included Brent, Blair, Brian and Barry Cudmore, Sue Martin, and Dee Hudson, all of whom were to have a long history with Ponca Hills Farm, including as instructors, and also with the Nebraska horse industry.

Ponca Pony Club participated in a 1974 Regional Rally at Fort Leavenworth, KS which the B team won by "a wide margin." The C2 team won for the second year and the C1 team came in 2nd. All considered it a great showing coming out of the chaos of hosting the National Rally earlier.

Jim Urban and Janalee Salestrom achieved A rating by the end of 1975. The club had 11 B rated riders: Tammy Cudahy, Stacy Godfrey, Jon Ketzler, Beth Maenner, Patti Miller, Sharon Naughton, Jim Urban, Sue Gidney, Valerie Grauer, Sue Martin and Janalee Salestrom..

Most of juniors riding at Ponca in the early 70s were involved in Pony Club and the club frequently invited veterinarians and other horse experts to do programs at Ponca. Pat Rothe, an adult boarder, loved to sit in on these presentations. She says the Pony Club sessions were a major source of her learning about horses.

Club Boosted by an Active Group of Parents

Figure 23. Vem Salestrom, DC of Ponca Pony Club for over a decade, with beginning Pony Club member and the Ponca's favorite "Miss Margaret."

Pony Club parents are critical to the success of an organization. The Ponca Pony Club developed a core group of parents who did the work and became good friends. Pulled into service by kids who were spending large amounts of time with horses, the parents organized group mounted lessons and study sessions. They ran meets and rallies, transported kids to "Know Downs" (now called Quiz Rallies) and learned to drive trailers to take horses and riders to regional meets. At Ponca they helped build jumps and hunt coops and supplied a continual supply of food and snacks. At regional meets, they volunteered as jump crew, hospitality organizers, and all the various stations needed for jumping and flat classes.

"Come on Out and Horse Around." That was the title of the Stars and Stripes Charity Horse Show, July 1-4, 1982. It involved a major effort by Ponca Pony Club parents, who organized, publicized, secured sponsorships, and ran the competition. A benefit for the U.S.

Equestrian Team, it was held at Christensen Field in Fremont. The show was recognized by AHSA, INHJA, and the Midwest Grand Prix Association.

The event drew riders from all over the country and even Mexico. Ponca had a large group of riders (and horses) including: Lisa Yanney (Tosca and Mary Jean), Sue Martin (Count Your Blessings and Annie Oakley), Jan Mactier (Hialeah, Icarus, and Sentimental Journey), Dee Hudson Slagle (Pac Man and Go Lightly), Hillary Horner (Daddy's Paycheck), Jeff Johnson, (Cinnabar), Jane Kasner (Friendly Persuasion), Robyn Eden (Sgt. Crocker), Krystal Seitzinger (Sassafrass), Karman Seitzinger (Dionysian Dream and Zeichen Hier), Brian Cudmore (Damion, Little John and the Saint), Brent Cudmore (Country Boy and Black Jack), and Pat Rothe (Pipe Dream).

Figure 24. The Stars and Stripes Charity Horse Show was a huge undertaking by the parents of Ponca Pony Club.

Omaha Veterinarian Dr. Smalley and his wife Paula were active parents with Jenny, Jon and Sandy in Pony Club in the early 1980s. Dr. Smalley remembers both the kids and parents which were, in his opinion: "The greatest group of parents and kids. They all pitched in and it was a wonderful experience for all of them."

Over the years Dr. Smalley gave dozens of training sessions on horse health, anatomy, and care to Pony Clubbers. Member Kirk

Figure 25. From left, back row: Kay Salestrom, Jon Smalley, Jeff Johnson, Vem Salestrom, Leslie Hansen Thompson, Liz Lamphier, Cheryl Cook. Front row: Sara Hansen, Kirk Wagner, Katie Tinsman, Jaymes Salestrom, Jayson Seitzinger, Dana Miller, Karman Seitzinger, team manager (kneeling).

Wagner remembers watching as Dr. Smalley set a puppy's broken leg after a horse stepped on it. The Wagners adopted the puppy after much pleading from Kirk and sister Kirstin.

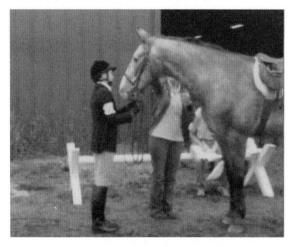

Figure 26. Sandy Smalley and Chipmunk Pony Club Testing - Horse Management.

Paula Smalley particularly remembers the summer of 1983 when eight Pony Club members worked the whole summer to prepare for their B rating. The testing was held at Ponca Hills Farm and "getting them ready was a huge effort by both parents and kids," she said.

"Many of the kids had their own horses and rode or trailered them over to Ponca. The Mactiers' were so generous, never charging for use of the cross-country course or arena. It was a huge thing they did for those kids," Paula said. "Jan (Mactier) was just a kid herself, but she was out there, giving those kids lessons to get them ready." Paula said Kay Salestrom also helped coach the kids all that summer.

Kirstin Wagner, Lisa Yanney, Krystal Seitzinger, Leslie Hansen, Hillary Horner, Jane Kasner, Elizabeth Lamphier and Sandy Smalley all earned B ratings in the fall of 1983, a record number testing for an extensive and highly advanced test on both mounted and horse knowledge.

The Smalleys chaperoned a group attending a Rally in Des Moines. Unsubstantiated rumor has it that there was a tornado warning. Dr. Smalley, a Californian, graduate of UC Davis Veterinary School, was unused to tornado warnings. Wisely he got under a table in the motel basement with the kids while the other parents, Nebraska natives, were unruffled.

Pony Club Graduates Remember

Tom Caniglia, a charter member of Pony Club, recently commented on a Ponca Facebook page of pictures of kids in summer camp: "Without Ponca Hills I wouldn't be half the person I am."

Figure 27. Pony Clubbers from left, Lindy Stratbucker on Take It Easy, Lori Patterson on Bambi, Mike Blose on Jack Tar; and Brent Cudmore on Lots of Fun. Missy Martin (front) was Stable Manager.

Lisa Yanney remembers getting her B rating at Ponca: "Realizing the day before my "B" test that I'd never ridden the horse I was using for cross-country. With a storm approaching, Jan (Mactier) hopped on Hilalea and I on my test mount, Charlie. We picked up a gallop straight from the mounting block, jumped the entire cross-country course without so much as slowing to a trot because the thunder was rolling and the sky darkening. We pulled up in front of the barn just as the rain started to the sound of a lightening clap. It was something out of the movies. Then, during the test, everything ran late, and we only had time to jump a couple of cross-country jumps before the tester had to catch a flight."

Figure 28. Kirstin Wagner on her pony Jack Be Nimble testing for mounted rating. She achieved a B rating.

Kirstin Wagner started taking lessons at Ponca on school horses by age 7. Her parents, Judd and Pat Wagner and younger brother, Kirk, lived on an acreage on Shongasta Road, on the eastern border of Ponca Hills Farm. Later they had their own horses which they kept at their place. They rode over the hill to Ponca for lessons with Jan Mactier. Both were in Ponca Pony Club from 1977, early grade school, through high school and participated in many Ponca clinics. Kirstin especially remembers participating in a clinic with the famous George Morris. Pat Wagner said, "Kirstin had a Pony Club notebook at least six inches thick. The kids learned so much. For example, how to present themselves to adults. That's a big deal for kids. We felt it was a great experience for them and well worth the huge time commitment as well as the money. We felt we sent them to college twice."

Kirstin Wagner Crane shared her memories of Ponca and Pony Club: "I met my best friend in Pony Club. We both had notebooks that we'd decorated with stickers of horses and so, after a thorough comparison, we decided we'd be friends for life. And we are. In the summer, we rode our ponies all over Ponca Hills, swam with them in the Missouri River, played horseback hide-and-seek, and suffered through blistering nettles and endless mosquito bites. We sweated our way through Pony Club rallies and I do think our C-teams had a clean sweep of the ribbons one year. But I also remember disastrous dressage tests and horrendous refusals that were so unfortunately timed at rallies. But it didn't matter because we were sweating and getting sunburned as a team!

"I also remember winters in the barn during Pony Club meetings with feet so cold I thought they would shatter immediately upon dismount. I remember singing horse-themed Christmas carols (re-writing them to be horsey was a Pony Club activity). And of course, Mr. Mactier as Santa Claus on his giant, and patient, horse, Lara.

"Fall would mean eating apples picked directly off the trees while on horseback. My pony club friends and I would tuck in our t-shirts so that we could store as many apples as we could down our shirts creating very lumpy muffin tops. Disaster invariably struck when someone's shirttails wiggled loose, releasing an avalanche of apples over horse haunches.

"In the spring, we battled bees and slippery mud and created 'dream treat recipes' for our horses that involved lots of oats and molasses. We would also begin preparing for the next 'Know Down' by studying pony anatomy and quizzing each other on the merits of various fencing materials. And thrown in there somewhere would be a square dance at the barn, where we drank too much soda and ate too many popsicles.

"I think I still have scars from those mosquito bites, but the memories and friends I made during Pony Club made all that calamine lotion worth it."

Figure 29 At age 8, Kirk Wagner rode the cross-country course on his pony Artful Dodger. He broke his arm when the Dodger dodged a jump and Kirk took it without him.

Kirstin's younger brother Kirk Wagner's recollections reflect the fun young boys had: "Learning all about short-sheeting beds, swirlies, and prank wake-up calls while staying in a hotel at Know-Downs; massive dirt clod fights between events; being a barn rat and just exploring the stable- including places we weren't supposed to go; and we loved the pig roasts at Ponca stables."

Kirk remembers the learning experiences such as, "Breaking my arm on a cross-country course when I went over the fence and my pony (Artful Dodger) didn't; washing and conditioning tack and the smell of Murphy's soap; and watching Dr. Smalley de-worm a horse." And, of course, Kirk will never forget: "watching a foal being born at Ponca stables and making good friends with all the other pony clubbers."

Figure 30. Pony Club Team at National Rally at Abbe Ranch, CO, 1981. From left, Mary Cannon on Trapper, Kirstin Wagner on Shiloh, Hillary Horner on Snowball, Krystal Seitzinger on Schatze. Liz Cannon is stable manager.

Karman, Krystal and Jayson Seitzinger were members of Pony Club in the late 70s and 80s. Their parents, Lyle and Sherma, who got involved in support of their kids, were active both as Pony Club parents and as members of the North Hills Hunt. Sherma was a DC of Ponca Pony Club and a longtime treasurer of the Hunt and Lyle became a Master of Foxhounds. Karman, Krystal and Jayson rode on the Hunt staff as whips. Krystal earned her Pony Club A rating in 1986.

The Seitzinger kids rode their horses from their acreage on Northern Hills Drive (near 72nd street) to Ponca. It was at least three miles over numerous large hills and across Highway 75. "Through Pony Club, the kids were instructed in staying safe around 1100-pound animals and how to properly prepare their horses for a show or hunt. They learned that they need to water, feed and care for their horses before they feed themselves," Sherma said.

Merrilee Hansen, just out of college, began boarding a horse at Ponca in 1967 and joined the North Hills Hunt. Her two daughters,

Leslie and Sara, started in Pony Club in 1979 and were members from grade school through high school. "They learned to take responsibility and the importance of safety," she said. Her kids learned so much about the correct way of handling and caring for horses. "I think the horse

Figure 31. Sara Hansen Age 9, D rating, at Pony Club competition in 1979.

reflects what the rider is giving him," Merrilee said.

Merrilee's daughter, Sara Hansen Shedd, started in Pony Club and lessons at age 9, remembers Ponca Pony Club: "It's difficult to quantify when that was your life and you just were in it living it and loving it. I remember not being able to blow gum bubbles at some event (gymkhana or something??) Mostly I remember getting bucked off a lot. Heat stroke. Good friends. What was the horse- gymnastics-vaulting thing called? A million tadpoles in the water jump. Leon the Peon. Baby birds falling out of the rafters. The sand in the arena and you can't run fast through it. Running at magical speed down the aisles: never have I run as fast as that! Climbing up the inside of the cabinets that held all the pony club stuff and eating lunch on top of them in the rafters. Hide and seek – hiding in the attic above the far tack room and no one EVER found me. The most perfect ice-cold water in the tack room. Lovely raw carrots. Put your heels down. Galloping at high speeds with no fear. Airborne, a.k.a. 'Burnt Air' per Ned. Eating the sugar out of clover flowers. Trying to get your horse to come in from the paddock."

Figure 32. Pony Club From left, Colleen Quinn, Jayme Salestrom, Liz Cannon help build jumps for upcoming rally.

Leslie Hansen Thompson, Sara's older sister, lives on a ranch in Montana and raises quarter horses, Australian Shepherds, and Maine

Coon Cats. She earned a B Level. Leslie, the "best friend" Kirstin Wagner mentioned, wrote:

"Pony Club and the horses saved me. I was a country girl stuck in a big city school, and while I had some school friends, I could never really be myself with them. I always felt I had to be dressed nice, worried about 'fitting in' and just the basic, massive insecurities of most young girls. I was not happy. I was lonely. But ahhh! My horse friends in Pony Club saw me filthy dirty, sweaty, laughing my head off, daring, scared, adventurous, and for some reason that I still can't explain, nobody ever cared a bit who looked like what or where they came from, who was popular or not...I had found my 'tribe' and everything changed. I was, finally, happily MYSELF."

Figure 33. DCs Vern Salestrom (right) and Sherma Seitzinger. Vern served as DC for over a decade and both had three kids in Ponca Pony Club.

"I remember picking apples, standing ohh-so-carefully on my pony's back to reach the best ones… tucking in my shirt and filling it with red gems…which of course – one for me, one for the horse, one for me… all the way home!"

"The Know Downs and rallies….my first real taste of freedom from the parents! The endless studying stuff I could probably still quote word for word today, all these long years later! Come on, you ALL know it! Colic: spasmodic, impacted, or twisted! I can still wrap a horse leg with the best of 'em! We made miles-long human cross-country jumping courses after the riding lessons, in the middle of July then ran them till heatstroke was imminent, saved by a freezer full of fudge sickles! Then on to the 'stadium jumping and dressage' (all done on our human feet) and Lord help you if you 'cantered' on the wrong lead!"

Lisa Yanney joined Ponca Pony Club in 1979 as a 13-year-old. She remembers, "My little pom pom topped caliente helmet cover always blew off and I rode around in the functional equivalent of a skull cap." Lisa's memories of Pony Club include, "Buying boxes of diapers as a young teen and explaining to the checkout clerk that I was going to use them to protect my horse from nails in her stall, and carefully using electrical tape to put green and white stripes on everything I owned from hoof pick to galloping boots so our team equipment was easily identifiable."

Vem Salestrom was DC and Joint DC of Ponca Pony Club for 11 years from 1975 - 1985, the Club's longest serving District Commissioner, with three of her children participating and becoming A rated members. She has a reputation for her creativity in coming up with new projects and innovative ways for the kids to learn the huge amount of information they needed to compete in Know Downs. Vem's daughter, Janalee, received an A rating in 1975 along with Jim Urban. Kay Salestrom received her A rating in 1982.

Vem's son Jaymes Salestom earned his B Rating in 1988 and HA in 1989. He and Jayson Seitzinger were close friends and did everything together. Jaymes continued to ride as an adult for many years and served as Huntsman and Master of Foxhounds for the Gamble Hills Hounds and Wabash Hounds.

USET coach, Col. Bengt Ljungquist came to Ponca to give a clinic about 1979. He had guided the U.S. dressage team to a bronze medal at the 1976 Olympics and a gold medal at the 1975 Pan American Games. He was appointed coach for the US Equestrian Team for dressage and was always on the lookout for talent. A-Rated pony club member, Janalee Salestrom, took the clinic. She was noticed. A try-out for the team was held in Chicago at Wayne DuPage Stables and Janalee made the "long list" for the team. She was invited to train

Figure 34. Colonel Bengt Ljungquist devoted a decade to furthering dressage in the United States, including at Ponca. He developed a judges' training program that continues today and conducted the first organized forums.

for a week with Ljungquist at the Diamond Jim Brady Estate in Hillsbrough, N.J. She made a good showing; but, unfortunately, she did not make the cut to the "short list."

By the mid 1980s Leslie Hansen, Hillary Horner, Jane Kasner, Elizabeth Lamphier, Krystal Seitzinger, Kirstin Wagner and Lisa Yanney were all B rated riders. Dana and Kara Miller, children of active hunt members Dennis and Vera Miller, were just getting started in Pony Club. The Hansens, Wagners, Lamphier, O'Brians, Seitzingers, Smalleys, Wagners, Julie Kraw and Kim Peters were all part of the club as were their parents.

Krystal Seitzinger remembers traveling to a Pony Club Know Down Rally and "explaining to the hotel manager how an errant water balloon set off the room's fire alarms." At mounted rallies, Krystal, who had an A Rating by 1986, helped in judging the younger riders. She noted that the older riders at rally used the same perfectly clean extra tack for the entire team's tack check after the cross-country competition. "Yes, I knew them personally and they may or may not have been involved in the earlier water balloon incident," she laughed. The water balloon team went on to win the Regional Know Down and then represented Ponca at the National Rally.

Lisa Yanney, who earned her A rating in 1984, said, "I went to my A test in Seattle and they gave me a randomly drawn horse. I got a sheet of paper telling me about him, so I went to groom and tack him up. I was cleaning his tail when he fell asleep in the cross ties. His head drooped and he hit the ties, woke up, freaked out, broke the cross ties and promptly fell over, cutting himself in several places. Folks came running to see what had happened and the barn manager casually said, 'Oh, he always does that.' Really, why not mention it on the piece of paper? Anyway, we covered him in Furacin and off we went. I was riding him for the dressage phase and the assignment was to ride the horse and then present him to the testers for sale, showing off his strengths. We were warming up in a big field before going into the dressage ring and every time I would ask for the canter, he'd pick up the wrong lead. Fortunately, with no rail, I just turned in the direction of his lead and faked it. Finally, I just decided to ask him with the 'wrong' leg and he picked it up beautifully. I think that was one of the main things Pony Club taught me was to just figure things out. Deal with whatever happens and make it work. Good life lesson, really!"

Members Graduate, New Ones Join 1985 - 2000

Figure 35. Ponca Team took first place at 1991 Midwest Rally.

Jan Redick took over as DC in 1986 and the members included Michelle Atwood, Kristin Bachman, Susie Gordon, Julie Morrow, Greg Queal, Melinda Redick, Seitzingers, Smalleys and Wagners. Carrie and Tracy Johnson. Justin Queal joined the next year. (Greg and Justin Queal are sons of Sally Gaucasana Queal, who taught lessons at Ponca for many years and then established "The Riding Center," across the street. Greg Queal runs that barn today and continues to board horses and give lessons.) Jim Urban started the Northern Hills English Riding Academy located at Ponca.

Elizabeth Hoffmaster joined the Club in 1988. At that time many of the higher rated riders had left for college and the newer members of the club were aided by the B and C level riders such as

Susie Gordon, (C1) Elizabeth Lamphier (HA), Shelly and Tina O'Brien, (C3s) Kim Peters (C3), Greg Queal (C1), Jayson Seitzinger (C3), Lisa Teske (C3) and Jaymes Salestrom (B).

In 1992-93, Kim Peters, Jaymes Salestrom, and Lisa Teske earned A ratings and Jennifer Beatty, Laura Perry, Lisa Hinder, and Jami Smith earned B ratings. Kim Peters Barone said, "When I started riding at 11 yrs. old, my trainer, Jim Urban, operated a lesson program out of Ponca. I rode there until he opened his own farm, Quail Run Horse Centre. My fondest memories of Ponca were of enjoying all the beautiful property it had to offer! I enjoyed participating in the Ponca Hills Hunt on my medium pony. We had so much fun galloping across the fields following the hounds on a chase. I also loved to jump the cross-country jumps in lessons and trail riding all around the property."

"Jim encouraged all his riders to be well rounded and loved the horsemanship that Pony Club valued," Kim said. "My favorite memory of Ponca Hills Pony Club was the opportunity I had to compete in the National Pony Club Festival in Kentucky. After the competition was over, there were several top clinicians available for lessons and non-mounted activities. It was such a special weekend for me to be able to see the people that I had read about in the Chronicle of the Horse."

After 2000, Ponca Pony Club membership numbers declined significantly. This is largely due to the tremendous demands on high school age kids. Pony Club advanced riders are expected to help the younger riders while working to test for their own advancement in Pony Club. Lessons, horse shows, and school activities and studies leave them little time left for the rigorous demands of Pony Club. In addition, both parents working means they have less time and flexibility, especially if they have several children involved in different activities.

As one A rated rider, now in her 50s, lamented, "Unfortunately we are turning out riders rather than horsemen. They compete on expensive horses with trainers who coach them into winning in rated shows, but they don't have the knowledge of the horse and horse care and are less able to figure rides out for themselves."

Fortunately, Pony Clubs are strong nationally and continue to offer kids a tremendous opportunity. "Young riders learn discipline, attention to detail, responsibility and teamwork at a level available only in the military," one Pony Club father said at a Rally in 2015. He said his oldest daughter breezed through college and medical school as a result of the approach to learning she acquired in Pony Club.

Today the Ponca Ponca Club sends several teams to Quiz Rally (knowledge competition formerly called Know Downs) and Mega Rally (horse care and stable management and mounted competition). It still depends on dedicated parents and helpful barns to supply and transport horses. Quail Run, Jim Urban and his family's hunter jumper facility, sponsors the club currently. Lincoln's Cornhusker Pony Club is very active and sponsors "Games" competitions, attracting kids from farms in several communities.

Pony Club Graduates Make a Lifetime of Horses

Pony Club Members who achieve A or B ratings have a thorough knowledge of horse care and management and ride at a level qualifying them as instructors. Many of the graduates of Ponca Hills Pony Club went on to make careers in the horse industry and continue to pass on their knowledge and skills to the next generations. They are part of the legacy of excellence that Ponca Hills Farm created: people inspired by classical training in riding who believe in perpetuating the best the sport has to offer.

Ponca's first A rated member, Jan Mactier Moriarty, had a full riding career and taught lessons at Ponca Hills Farm, which today she owns and manages. She actively supports an international driving team, Team Landhope, with Allison Stroud from Unionville, PA. Jan serves the team as Director of Operations and Videographer when the team is on the road and showing nationally and internationally. She started with the team in 2003, first with Connemara 4-Pony Team, then in 2014, with a 4-Horse Team of Gelderlanders.

Nancy Zandbergen Wilson and her husband founded a camp for boys and girls in Flat Rock, NC in 1991 called Camp Wayfarer. It is a traditional camp offering a huge variety of activities including riding. They use their own horses but also use the University of South Carolina's NCAA horses, old equitation, hunters and jumpers donated to the school. Nancy is past president of the Tryon Riding and Hunt Club, which partners with the Tryon International Equestrian Center and helped start the Carolinas' Show Hunter Hall of Fame in 2017. "I have ridden and shown my whole life in the amateur hunters and now have returned to eventing which is so much fun. I am still riding daily, bringing along a few green ones and selling one here and there, especially the ones we have bred and raised," Nancy said.

Jon Ketzler is an anesthesiologist and critical care doctor at the University of Wisconsin, Madison. He continues to actively participate in Three-Day Eventing at the Preliminary level. His wife Mary, also an anesthesiologist, also rides in Three-Day Events. They live on a farm with a cross-country jumping course and a collection of aging horses, donkeys, pigs, and rescued dogs.

The four Cudmore boys grew up doing Pony Club, eventing, fox hunting, pony jumpers and "a bit of everything else." They all rode with North Hills Hunt. Brent Cudmore, the oldest, moved his horses and students to Ponca Hills Farm in 2011 following a Missouri River flood which devastated Glencarry Stables. At Ponca he teaches and trains. Barry Cudmore is in the horse transport business in California.

Brian Cudmore, an accomplished rider, suffered a massive heart attack and died while riding a green jumper in a show in Canada. He was in his early 40s. North Hills Hunt in 2003 created the Brian Cudmore Memorial Plate, awarded to high point jumper rider in all level four and above classes at the NHH horse show.

Blair Cudmore became the youngest North Hills Hunt member to earn his colors, at age 13. He established a Holsteiner breeding program and sells his horses from coast to coast. He has some of the top Holsteiner brood mares and stallions in the country. His wife Karen and their daughter Brooke are top competitors in the show jumping arena. Karen was often a member of the Canadian Show Jumping Team, competing nationally and internationally. They own Heartland Farms, which has a large show jumping and training barn near Elk City, NE and numerous other properties around the greater Omaha area where they raise, train and ride show horses. A Chronicle of the Horse feature article on Blair and Karen Cudmore, (March 18, 2013) quoted trainer and a former longtime Heartland staffer Kris Killam: "I don't know anyone else in America who's produced as many international level jumpers as Blair and Karen, from the ground up."

Leslie Hansen raises quarter horses, Australian Shepherds and Maine Coon cats on a cattle ranch in Montana. Her breeding program stresses disposition. "Nowadays the leg wrapping is more likely applied to my children's hurts, or the dog. My passion for riding has continued far beyond my B rating, but the foundation from Pony Club has never failed me. I moved to Montana, threw over the English saddle for a Western one, and have realized my dream of raising horses. I am married now to a rancher; I am teaching my children to love horses. Moving the cattle, scrounging through the mountain meadows and timber, over hills and valleys, through rivers and snow to gather the cattle. There are times when I have been so busy, such as when the children were very young, I would forget and wonder why were people so obsessed with horses? Why was I? Pony Club and all the rest seemed so long ago.....and then one warm spring day I find myself unraveling the wind knots from my horses' manes and currying off the last bit of winter...smell the horse scent mixed with sunshine...have that massive beast turn his head to me in peace and trust.....and I know again why."

Jim Urban, who grew up showing, riding and hunting at Ponca, went on to build Northern Hills English Riding Academy, located at Ponca Hills Farm. Later, with wife Patrice, his former riding student, he established Quail Run Horse Center in Elkhorn, NE. Together, with their three sons, they run Quail Run and also own Urban Events which sponsors A rated horse shows in Iowa and Nebraska. Jim continues with a busy schedule of teaching and coaching the Pony Club teams. Son Dan rides, trains and teaches while running and organizing Urban Events. Son Tom is farm manager at Quail Run and occasionally (and very successfully) competes. Tom's wife Danee is one of Quail Runs trainer/instructors. Son Mike travels all over the U.S. managing jump crews. All three boys were members of Ponca Pony Club.

Lisa Yanney Roskens, who rode and attended clinics at Ponca, went on to establish her own Far Hills Farm within a mile of Ponca. A well-respected amateur jumper rider, she founded the Omaha Equestrian Foundation, designed to bring international caliber show jumping to the Midwest. Her International Omaha event, held annually at the CHI Health Center Arena, draws some of the best jumpers in the

Figure 36. Lisa Yanney Roskens on Jan Moriarty's new Dutch Warmblood, Officer (aka Joy), at Ponca's indoor arena. Lisa, an A Rated Pony Clubber, pitched in to ride as Jan had two young children at home. The training was successful. The horse sold for $100,000.

country to compete each April, culminating in speed jumping and Grand Prix competitions. Her vision and ability to mobilize a highly talented volunteer force and attract sponsorships led to the 2017 FEI World Cup championships in both show jumping and dressage brought to Omaha. Her daughter Mary is taking after her mom, working her way up the ranks from ponies to the equitation and the junior jumpers. She qualified for the USEF Medal Finals in Harrisburg, PA in 2018 and the ASPCA Maclay Regionals and now is focused on jumpers.

Kim Peters Barone now owns and runs Raven Ridge Farm, a hunter/jumper training facility outside of Minneapolis MN. She specializes in breeding, producing, training, coaching and competing top hunters and jumpers.

Sue Hull served as DC of Ponca Pony Club for over a decade starting in 2001. She remains active today as part of the "Masters" program which she organized as a part of Ponca Pony Club. Masters was started by USPC for adults (many PC parents) who missed out on Pony Club and wanted to participate. Sue's son Matt, Ponca Pony Club A rated, graduated from Veterinary School at Kansas State University. He still participates in US Pony Club, testing young riders working to achieve higher levels of certification.

Please see Appendix for listing of:
- Ponca Pony Club District Commissioners (DCs)*
- Ponca Pony Club members achieving A or B rating by year*

*Listings after 2000 are included on-line on the United States Pony Club web site.

Ponca Hills Farm — A Half Century of Memories

Riders Recognized in Local and Regional Shows

As Ponca riders and horses advanced in their training, they participated in horse shows. The big fenced-in grass ring, on the south side of the barn across the driveway, and the outdoor sand ring were the scene of several horse shows recognized by the American Horse Shows Association (later to become the US Equestrian Federation) in the late 60s and 70s.

Figure 37. The first shows at Ponca were held in the fenced in ring south of the barn. Allan Mactier takes his horse over a jump in preparation for one of the first shows.

Separate hunter/jumper shows were held throughout the Midwest at such venues as the American Royal complex in Kansas City and individual hunter barns. Several Ponca Hills Farm riders made names for themselves as top equitation, hunter and jumper riders, including the Cudahy sisters, Tammy and Nina.

Ponca Hills Farm began hosting its own hunter/jumper show each year, utilizing the big grass ring south of the main barn as well as the lower sand ring. The Mactiers wanted to bring the fun and excitement of showing hunters and jumpers to a venue in Nebraska and be a show destination for riders competing throughout the Midwest in Iowa, Minnesota, Kansas and Missouri.

Horse shows at Ponca Hills Farms were typical of shows of that time – usually three-day shows beginning on a Friday and continuing through the weekend, with riders showing in two divisions plus the equitation classes. There were many open jumper classes. Jan Moriarty remembers, "The junior and equitation classes were packed, and there was an amazing amount of camaraderie which spawned genuine friendships – and there were lots and lots of talented and well-loved horses."

The Mactiers and other horse enthusiasts in the Omaha area were united in their support for the Omaha Charity Horse Show in the 60s. Held annually at the old Ak-Sar-Ben Coliseum, it show-cased a multitude of breeds and dis-ciplines, attracting large audiences to watch jumpers, hunters, three- and five-gaited Saddlebreds, fine harness horses and ponies, along with Tennessee Walkers, Shetlands, parade horses and Hackneys in a variety of classes, and showcasing a wide variety of riding styles and breeds in one entertaining package. It was "A Rated" by the American Horse Shows Association in four divisions: Five Gaited, Three Gaited, Western Pleasure, and Open Jumpers. It was rated "B" in Fine Harness, Walking Horse, and Roadster.

Figure 38. The Ak-Sar-Ben Charity Horse Show brought riders of all disciplines together. The show had major involvement of Allan Mactier, Phil Durbrow, and others at Ponca Hills Farm.

The show involved other local horsemen, such as Abe Baker, the Clarence Landons and the Dr. Hal Giffords. The show also brought in big-name entertainment along with the show horses, delighting horse lovers of all ages with one big entertainment package. The show included a formal dinner party.

The year Allan Mactier was Chairman, assisted by Phil Durbrow, the event featured a special exhibition of the Royal Canadian Mounted Police and received a front-page article in Horse World. The event had over 700 entries that year, a record for the show. Jan rode her horse Christopher Robin that year.

The only problem Allan had with the Charity Horse Show was that too much money went into prize money and not enough to charities!

The executive board included many Ponca and North Hills Hunt people including Allan Mactier, Dr. Paul Mooring, and Philip Durbrow in 1968. Heading fund raising efforts were Arthur Pinkerton, Taylor Snow, and Abe Baker. Other Ponca/North Hills Hunt members in charge included Mrs. Charles Bonniwell, Mrs. Helmuth Dahlke, Donovan Ketzler, and Mrs. Roger Duhnke.

Participants included many from the Ponca Pony Club as well as North Hills Hunt. Nancy Zandbergen aboard Tom Caniglia's horse Cricket posted a perfect round to win the Pony Jumping, the first year that class was offered.

The Omaha Charity Horse Show was discontinued in 1968. The North Hills Hunt, which had its own division in the show, decided that they wanted a show as an annual event every May, that would be registered and rated with the American Horse Show Association (AHSA). Early venues were Ponca Hills Farm, Christensen Field Fremont, and later, Glencarry Stable in Crescent, Iowa.

The North Hills Hunt Horse Show was designed to bring together the fox hunting and horse show constituents to support one another and foster cross-disciplinary cooperation. It included "Qualified Field Hunter" divisions. This worked well since this was a time when people did literally everything with their horses, from fox hunting, to eventing, to horse shows. Trainers emphasized a proper background in basic dressage, and the hunter courses often consisted of galloping over rolling hills and jumping "off your eye," not counting strides in the lines in a confined arena. Trainers at that time appreciated the forward momentum fox hunting tends to give a horse. Again, Ponca Hills Farm provided an ideal place for training cross-country.

Learn from the Best - Instructors at Ponca

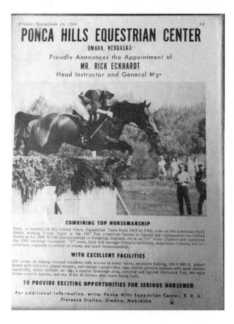

Figure 39. An early poster promoting Ponca Hills Farm featured Rick Eckhardt.

Ponca Hills Farm was not just another riding stable or a place where you took a few casual lessons or just jumped on a horse. Ponca was where you came to learn to do it right. This philosophy resulted from a combination of men with military training and a woman, Ann Mactier, with an inherited commitment to education and a philosophy: "Anything worth doing is worth doing well."

Determined to offer the best instruction and learning opportunities, Ann sought ways to bring new young riders into the sport and to expose them to the best examples of horsemanship possible. That was why she insisted on top quality instructors and bringing a variety of renowned clinicians to the barn on a regular basis. Riders, she felt, needed to see the best if they were to aspire to be the best.

When you learned how to do it right, you could have fun, and be safe doing it. Discipline was emphasized as was correct attention to detail. You didn't come to a lesson with untucked shirt or dirty boots. As instructor Rick Eckhardt put it: "If you look sloppy, you think sloppy. If you think sloppy, you ride sloppy. And if you ride sloppy, you get hurt." (See Appendix "Why All the Rules?")

—World-Herald News Service Photo.

Pan-Am Champ Becomes Omahan

Rick Eckhardt of North Fork, Va., former member of the United States Equestrian team and a gold medal winner in the 1967 Pan-American Games, has been named general manager and head riding instructor at Ponca Hills Stable. Eckhardt, 22,- was a member of the United States team the last two years in both national and international competition. The gold medal came in the Pan-Am Games in Winnepeg.

Figure 40. Rick Eckhardt taught at Ponca, in the mid 70s. He was responsible for attracting internationally known riders to give clinics.

As a result, riders took pride in themselves, their horses and their barn. In the burgeoning show horse industry of the 1960s and 70s, Ponca Hills Farm's reputation for excellence spread throughout the Midwest and extended to the coasts. Ponca was not just a barn and riding arenas. The farm expanded to offer cross-country opportunities in its forested hills. Allan was a master at planning trails to give riders the most beautiful views through the forest, around ponds, and across meadows. He also loved to offer riders excitement and experience using the natural hills, ditches and downed trees.

Figure 41. Phil Durbrow built jumps and encouraged young riders to ride outside on hills and across meadows. Pictured from right, are Jan Mactier on Hireath; Durbrow on Alibi Bart; Mindy Nance on Kelby and Deb McKinnon.

Ponca also gained the attention of others already experienced in the sport like Phil Durbrow, who appeared just after the barn was built. Phil had worked with the Olympic Three-Day Event team and rode horses for one of the leading show jumping families, the Galvins. Phil had designed the national Three-Day trials course at Pebble Beach, CA, where Dick Collins was manager, and had won the US Nationals when he was only 16.

Durbrow immediately became a fixture at Ponca and spent most of his spare time building jumps and coaching kids. "Philip enjoyed building cross-country jumps," Jan Moriarty said. "He built jumps and taught us kids riding lessons. He did this in his free time and for his own enjoyment. There was no formal arrangement. Because of Phil we had, from the beginning, standards of excellence."

"How fortunate it was for all of us," Jan said. "He was an encyclopedia of information and experience. He had contacts with top echelon of the horse world at that time and was a Pied Piper for all the young people and adults."

He designed Ponca's first cross-country course (originally in the area which is now Hawk Wood Circle) in 1967. Parents of Pony Club members pitched in to help build jumps. He coached the first team headed to the Pony Club Rally in Kansas City in 1967.

Durbrow explained, "When I learned that Ponca was at the highest point in the county, I decided to build a tall jump at the highest point, so I could say we have a jump that is the highest in the county, and that is why 'Phil's Hill' was built - with the tolerance of the Mactiers." 'Phil's Hill' is still standing in Ponca's highest pasture, on the south side of the entrance to the farm.

Jan Moriarty said, "Phil is totally responsible for my parents' connection to Ireland and fox hunting. He introduced them to Dick Collins, founder of Pony Clubs on the West Coast. They became friends of Collins and his wife Marguerite and traveled with them and Phil to Ireland to fox hunt a couple of weeks a year. In Ireland, they became friends with Thady Ryan, legendary founder of the Scarteen Black and Tan Hounds with kennels near Tipperary. Pony Club in Nebraska can be credited to Phil introducing Mom to Dick Collins."

Durbrow worked at Nebraska Consolidated Mills and was greatly missed when he left Omaha in 1969 to attend Harvard Business School. Before he left he sought out and arranged hiring of Rick Eckhardt, a member of Pan Am Gold Medal USA Eventing Team. Rick won team gold at the 1967 Winnipeg, Canada Pan American Games in eventing with teammates Michael Page, J. Michael Plumb and James Wofford. Eckhardt arrived in the fall of 1968 and was in charge of riding and teaching at Ponca for a number of years.

Pony Club "A" Rider Nancy Zandbergen Wilson remembers, "When Rick Eckhardt was hired by the Mactiers I was committed to Ponca and all he gave us. He was tough, but so knowledgeable. All of us junior riders thrived under his tutelage. Rick brought all of us to a new level of riding for sure."

Rick came to Omaha from Glastonbury, CT. Ann Shepherd and Tom Ordway, who knew Eckhardt in Connecticut, also came as instructors. Tom came to be a working college student at UNO. Rick picked Tom up at the airport New Year's Day 1969 and brought him to the first "Zhivago" brunch at the Mactier home.

Figure 42. Allan Mactier (left) with Tom Ordway who was coaching teams at Pony Club Rally.

Ordway was an "A Rated" Pony Clubber. He won a National Rally on a B Team and showed at National Rally several times. He rode Nina Cudahy's Little Lucre at the National Rally in Nashville. Jan Moriarty recalls: "Tina's son Toby Cudahy accompanied Tom to help.

Tom told Toby to graze Lucre. I guess Toby got bored because when Tom returned, Toby was gone. Lucre was tied to the door handle of Brig. General Wing's T-Bird. Ordway said, 'Luck was with us as no one saw. I was dinged on stable management for leaving my saddle out in Sun.'" Ordway finished 2nd at Nashville in 1969, with the high score in the riding phases. He was winning the National Rally in Bath, Ohio in 1971 riding Nina Cudahy's Little Lucre, but he pulled out with concern over a possible (but minor) horse health concern. "Otherwise, Tom may have won National Rally as an A level rider," Jan said.

At Ponca, Tom rode horses, cleaned stalls, built jumps, plowed snow, anything that was needed. He became forever friends with Jan, Deb McKinnon, Bill Yates, John Grasmick, Stacy Adams, Mike Blose and others.

Jan Moriarty remembers riding in Lincoln with Lowell Boomer at the Pioneer Park Show with other hunter-jumper enthusiasts. They would all gather at Lee's restaurant for fried chicken after the show. "Dad always wanted more people to come," she said, "because more people meant more fun!"

Sue Martin came to Ponca, first taking riding lessons. Her sisters Julie and Missy were summer camp students and later helped with summer camps, taking campers up and down the "Piano" jump and enjoying the blackberries from the bushes there. Her brothers Sean and Pat also rode at Ponca. Pat worked with Mike Blose doing stalls, fences and haying and other odd jobs. Their mom established a tack shop, Horse Hardware, in what is now Ponca's office. In the fall of 1971, Sue became a working student for Ann Mactier and her summer camps. Jan Moriarty remembers, "Sue led summer campers up and down Ponca's hills, teaching them to walk up and trot down."

Figure 43. Sue Martin taught Ponca Summer Camp for many years.

"Sue Martin Wilde loves horses and she loves Ponca and Ponca loves Sue," Jan said. "For many years she has been a willing extra hand. Many times, she has taken on a horse as a project to train, doing clinics and shows…always resulting in an educated horse ready for sale or for other people to ride." Sue's role at Ponca continued to grow as she served as groom, trainer, and instructor, spanning over 40 years. Jan said, "You could put Sue in charge of anything." Sue even served as a babysitter for the Cudmore boys and lived in the yellow farmhouse at one time.

Ponca's early instructors also included Alex Adams, Gretchen Hennecke, Deb McKinnon, Sally and Corey Gaucasana, and Kay Buchanan. Michael Plumb, an exceptional instructor, came to Ponca in 1966. Merrilee Hansen remembered taking a lesson from him. "On my first dressage test, he had the courage to correct my turn out, which changed everything."

In 1971, Rick Eckhardt left Ponca for Topping Farm in Long Island, NY. Later Ordway, Deb McKinnon, and Tom Caniglia joined him. Allan was looking for someone to run the farm. John Grasmick, a good friend from the hunt, was attending a horse show near Minneapolis where he met Glenn Cudmore. Originally from Regina, Saskatchewan, Cudmore ran a competitive riding program in Winnipeg, Canada and was an international Three-Day Eventer. He had been on the Canadian Olympic Team. His wife, Carole, was an accomplished Dressage competitor.

Grasmick called Allan and Allan called Cudmore, who said he was not interested in moving to Omaha. But Allan was persistent. He checked the temperature in Omaha and Winnipeg and called Glenn back every few weeks on the coldest days. Allan, looking at the temperature in Omaha compared with that in Winnipeg, called Glenn when the spread was the greatest. That worked. Glenn said "Yes, we are coming." Glenn and Carole Cudmore and their four boys, Brent, Blair, Brian and Barry, moved to Omaha in 1972 to run Ponca Hills Farm and teach.

Figure 44. The Cudmore Family arrived from Canada in 1972 and moved into the yellow farmhouse. Pictured here soon after their arrival are from left, Brent, Blair, Carole, Brian, Glenn and Barry.

"They wanted me to get an apartment, but I told them I wouldn't run it (Ponca Hills Farm) if I didn't live on it," Glenn said. So, the family moved into the yellow farmhouse. Brent, the oldest, was 11 at the time of the move. All four boys started riding at Ponca and with the Pony Club. The Cudmores brought in horses as well as a man from Canada, Ned Tennis, who would handle the farming operation.

Carole Cudmore taught lessons to a few of the women who boarded at Ponca; but mostly, she was busy handling, riding and training the many Thoroughbreds which Glenn bought off the racetrack, as well as raising four boys. Glenn established a good business of buying, training and selling horses which he kept at Ponca. Everyone remembers Carole always had a broom in her hand, sweeping the aisles at the barn, friendly to all and chatting away through the clouds of dust from her broom.

The Cudmores managed Ponca Hills Farm for four years. "It was great," Glenn said. They left Ponca in 1976 to establish their own show barn, Glencarry, just across the river in Crescent, Iowa.

Rick Eckhardt arranged for George Morris to come and teach. He returned for 13 years on December 26 and often came for a second clinic in the summer. For many years, Ponca brought in two instructors a year, Gabor Foltenyi at Thanksgiving and Morris at Christmas.

Pat Rothe, a longtime boarder who started at Ponca in 1969, took lessons from both Glenn and Carole Cudmore, Alex Adams, Ann Shepherd, and from Dee Hudson, who came up from Lincoln to teach. She remembers taking a clinic with George Morris. Rothe also remembers internationally known instructors like Gordon Wright and Gabor Foltenyi doing dressage clinics. Austrian Karl Mikolka, former Chief Rider of the Spanish Riding School, came to Ponca to conduct a dressage clinic in 1978.

Figure 45. Dee Hudson, Lincoln, receives her first blue ribbon at Ponca Hills Farm, presented to her by Jon Ketzler, who later was Huntsman for the North Hills Hunt. His father, Donovan was a founder of the Hunt.

Merrilee Hansen started riding at Ponca in 1967 just after graduating from college. She rode with the Hunt in the early 70s. As her daughters Leslie and Sara grew, she was an active Pony Club mom. She herself favored dressage and participated in many clinics from some of the top riders Ponca brought in, including Karl Mikola, Jan Conant, Gordon Wright, Bengt Ljungquist, Gabor Foltenyi, and regularly trailered to Lincoln to ride with Lowell Boomer. In 1977 she taught the beginners at Ponca, always stressing safety.

She said, "I always wanted to keep the rider on top of the horse!"

Lincoln rider Dee Hudson recalls fondly her days riding at Ponca. "I remember the many clinics that I attended at Ponca. George Morris was someone that came early on, when I was around 14 years old. He was very hard on us and demanded the most out of us." Dee remembers: "Later came Karen Healey, Lisa Jaquin, and Archie Cox."

Figure 47. Van Ketzler trained WWII Cavalry recruits at Fort Riley. A founder of the North Hills Hunt, he felt military drills were great training for young riders at Ponca Hills Farm. Drills were conducted in the front pasture just south of the barn.

Lincolnites who regularly came to Ponca included the Hudsons, Mary Yates, a Lincoln dressage rider whose son Bill became a top event rider, Liz Aiken, Rollo Faulkner and John and Jewell Grasmick.

Figure 46. George Morris' student Karen Healey came from Thousand Oaks California to give jumping clinics at Ponca several times a year in the early 90s.

Figure 48. Archie Cox referred to the "Lincoln Logs" seen here at left. He referred to the large piles set into the indoor arena when two of the original trusses had to be replaced. He treated it as an outdoor experience indoors - just another obstacle. Rumor has it that Glenn Cudmore hid a TV inside the "logs" to watch the football game while judging schooling shows.

Archibald "Archie" Cox III came to Ponca from Southern California to conduct clinics between 1995 and 2012. He also came in December and was happy to know that one time he beat George Morris' record of teaching on the coldest day of the year. Cox said, "I have great memories of Ponca, Jan, Gary (Harnett), Kim Studdeman, Lisa Roskens, Dee Hudson and Pat Rothe and others. It was always fun in the indoor with the Lincoln Logs, the sand outdoor ring and of course jumping the banks and the water jump in the front field." Cox said he remembers "Sparrow, Ned, Reagan, Mario, X Man and so many more horses that helped to teach me what horses want and need. I always smile thinking of Ponca and Jan! Friendships and fantastic memories."

Jan was surprised and very pleased when, on one visit, Archie told her that Ponca is the only place he comes where the tack is always clean.

Figure 49. Archibald "Archie" Cox III, seen here on Dutch Warmblood Joy/Haagen-Dazs/ Officer, came to Ponca from Southern California to conduct clinics between 1995 and 2012.

Dee Hudson said, "I was so thankful that Jan was so generous, gracious, and caring, to bring such top horse people to Omaha, and allow us to be taught by them. Those of us that participated will never forget sitting and listening to them teach, on a beautiful day up on the hill above the riding arena. We all became better riders and are still passing on what we learned from them." Dee developed into a top Lincoln rider and one of Ponca's instructors in the late 90s. She wrote: "When my son Tanner was about a year old, I moved to Omaha with my fiancé, and Jan asked me if I could help out teaching lessons until she hired a fulltime trainer. I enjoyed training and teaching there, as I got to know some really wonderful people. I gave lessons to Charlotte Schenken, Susan MacQuiddy, Margie Hoffmaster, Bill McGinn, Fran Noble, Emily and Nancy Gordon, and a few others." Dee taught at Ponca for about two years, then moved back to Lincoln while her student, Amy Bender, took over as trainer.

Natalie Shaw's father, the internationally renowned transplant surgeon Byers "Bud" Shaw, was recruited to the University of Nebraska Medical Center in 1985 to set up the liver transplant program and serve as chief of transplantation. Her parents planned to stay just five years, but Dr. Shaw was persuaded to remain in Omaha when UNMC built a huge building as a centerpiece for its expanding transplant program. Natalie was born and grew up in Omaha and started taking riding lessons at Ponca at age 10. She took lessons through high school, starting with Stacey Diaz, and then from Kim Studeman and Erin Cardea. She grew in experience and then assisted the trainers, later becoming a full-time Ponca trainer.

Figure 50. Dee Hudson, from Lincoln, Showing at Ponca Hills Farm. Dee taught at Ponca for two years and she and her parents, Ann and Dick Hudson, have a longtime association with Ponca and North Hills Hunt. Jan called her "Dead Eye Dee" because she came into the arena adjusting her girth, talking, picking up a forward canter and have a perfect round. "She can see a distance from 10 - 15 strides out."

Other instructors at Ponca were Jack Mosley, Amy Bender, Martin Marcelli, George Schneider, Lisa Laralde, and Ann Carter, who left on graduation from law school. Linda McLaren, who came from William Woods, was the chief trainer and manager when she first came to Ponca.

Many of those who learned or instructed at Ponca have gone on to make their own mark on the equine industry, providing guidance and training to the next generation.

Sally Gaucasana Queal established The Riding Center, across the road from Ponca, where she taught for many years. Now her son Greg teaches and boards horses at the facility.

Figure 51. Martin Marcelli, a Ponca instructor, in a well-ordered tack room in the West Barn.

Tom Ordway continues as a popular clinician throughout the U.S. He grew up in South Glastonbury, CT and graduated from the Glastonbury Pony Club with an "A" rating before coming to Ponca.

Tom is a USEF R Technical Delegate at events across the country. He married Ponca Pony Club Charter Member and A Rated Debbie McKinnon in 1981. Together they run 100 Acre Farm in Princeton, ID. Deb is a retired Osteopath and Emergency Room physician. Tom teaches dressage, cross-country, and hunter jumper riding, and trains and sells sport horses. He was previously employed at a number of facilities including Ponca Hills Farm, Topping Riding Club, Sagaponick, NY, Leeward Farm, Millbrook, NY, and Maffitt Lake Farms, Des Moines, IA. Today he returns to Ponca every few months to conduct clinics.

Glenn Cudmore established Glencarry Stable in Crescent, IA in 1976. Glenn continued to buy, train and sell high quality horses. "At one time I could have furnished the entire Olympic Team," he said. The Cudmores had come to Ponca from Canada and they and their children and grandchildren have all contributed substantially to the horse industry in both countries. The four Cudmore sons went on to make their mark in the horse industry nationally and internationally. (See Pony Club Chapter: "PC Graduates Make a Lifetime of Horses.) After the major Missouri River flood in 2011 destroyed their facility, Glenn and Carole retired to Missouri Valley where they watch over broodmares for son Blair.

Dee Hudson taught in Lincoln after leaving Ponca and today lives with her husband Jack Mosier in Spaulding, NE where they raise cattle. In the middle of a cattle pasture, Dee has built a jumping arena with good footing for jumping and lights. There she teaches youngsters and junior riders who trailer in from many areas of the Sandhills. They are from cowboy country but love the opportunity to take English equitation and jumping. Dee often takes her young students to horse shows in Lincoln and Omaha.

Kristin Bachman went on to become a highly regarded event rider on the East Coast.

Figure 52. Mike Blose first started riding at Ponca Summer Camp at age 8. Fox Hunting, Pony Club, and summer jobs kept him at Ponca. A professional farrier, he has kept Ponca horses well-trimmed for over 40 years.

Mike Blose, son of Dr. Irvin Blose, whipped in for the North Hills Hunt and became a well-known farrier. Many of his customers are longtime friends who met him through Ponca Hills Farm. When Mike turned 16, he did an apprenticeship with farrier George Thallas, a former Army farrier, at the suggestion of his father. "Dad used to say good farriers and farmers who could make money are the only people he could respect," Mike said.

Mike worked as a farrier's apprentice and helped with haying until he was 18. In 1977, he went to farrier's school south of Lincoln and returned to Ponca a year later and continued as an apprentice. One day Allan Mactier told him, "I've got 80 horses for you to do."

In 1992, Mike suffered a serious head injury while shoeing a horse at Ponca. He recovered completely but in the approximately six months he couldn't work, farriers from all over this area trimmed and shod his clients' horses and turned the fees over to Mike. He still marvels at the camaraderie of the farriers to step in to help. Today Mike is still Ponca's farrier, taking care of the 60 plus horses at the farm.

Amy Bender, a trainer at Ponca, continues to teach young people and coach more advanced riders at Hampton Ridge Equestrian Center in Elkhorn. She was at Ponca when the movie crew filming "About Schmidt" came to film a few dream scenes. The crew was there for three days but only the school horse, Blizzard, made the cut and ended up in the film. A Ponca dog, Dexter, watched the movie making activities. The film crew was ecstatic as apparently a volunteer spectator dog signaled success for the movie's future.

Figure 53. Amy Bender taught at Ponca and later established her own school at Hampton Ridge Farm.

Natalie Shaw returned to Ponca after college, in 2012, and worked for Jan part-time. She was asked to teach the Ponca Summer Camp in June 2013 and then, starting with a few students, she gradually expanded her teaching load. She became the current full-time trainer and horse manager and moved into the yellow house on the property in 2014 where she lives with her dog Niner. She keeps a careful eye on the horses, checking them every night before shutting the barn

Ponca People, Managers and Traditions

Ponca hired many of the Pony Club kids to help with chores and haying. The Cudahy family was a fixture at Ponca for many years. Tammy Cudahy was working one summer at the barn, teaching, riding and helping with summer camp. A group of summer barn hands lived in a trailer where the little white house is now. Jan remembers, "They were called the Space Cowboys and included Tim Lauerman, Pat Martin (Sue Martin's brother) and Mike Blose. They weren't always awake when Tammy arrived for work, so she would walk into the trailer and throw a bucket of water on them to wake them up."

Figure 54. Allan as Santa on Georgie Girl gives Elizabeth Hoffmaster a ride at the Christmas party.

Mike Blose and Brent Cudmore remember doing farm chores and driving the big red tractor when they were 12 -14 years old. Mike recalls he was driving and hauling a big load of hay from the north pasture. Glenn Cudmore had some Angus cattle up there and a big bull came up from behind and butted the hay wagon. Brent Cudmore was up on top of the hay load. As the wagon started to turn over to the side, Mike remembers Brent running across the hay trying to stay on.

Santa arriving on a white horse was a fond memory of boarders at Christmas. "Santa" was definitely much taller and much less round than is legend, since it was Allan Mactier, riding Lara, a Cleveland Bay named after the lead in Dr. Zhivago. Santa Allan later rode Georgie Girl, a silver dapple grey, from England and then his great Chestnut, York.

Figure 55. Santa takes first grandchild, Mac Moriarty on his first Christmas and first ride at one month old.

Allan loved watching the kids taking care of their horses. He said, "When I die, I want to come back as a horse, with all these little girls brushing me and feeding me treats." On weekends, he often had breakfast with other riders at Harold's Cafe in Florence, where he ate breakfast about six days a week. Since that was before cell phones, he had his calls forwarded to the pay phone at Harold's. Allan usually returned with a sack of homemade donuts for the barn hands.

Allan, always looking to get more people out on the trails, started an annual New Year's Day "Ride to the River" in 1969. After a particularly beautiful ride to the river with Gretchen Giltner, they galloped across a snowy field, which reminded them of a popular movie. The New Year's morning ride was renamed the "Dr. Zhivago Ride" in 1970.

Figure 56. New Year's Day 2002 Zhivago ride. Only the most hearty joined that snowy day.

Everyone was invited to the ride from Ponca to N.P. Dodge Park and along the Missouri River. Frequently in deep snow, the pace was quick, led by Allan, and was highlighted by an all-out gallop across Walt Duda's large farm field. Allan led the group right down on the river sandbars, where only a few dared follow! Jan remembered her dad would say: "Anyone can stay up late celebrating New Year's Eve, but the real men get up early on New Year's Day and ride to the river!"

Riders and observers returned to the barn at noon to a traditional ham, black-eyed peas, cornbread and champagne breakfast. The tradition says that each black-eyed pea eaten on New Year's Day brings one day of good luck in the new year. The New Year's Day Zhivago Ride continues today, but those who turn out are a bit older, less daring and more social! The weather is always cold, and the brunch is always popular.

Pat Rothe started riding at Ponca in 1969 at age 22. After graduate school, Pat returned to Omaha and began taking tennis, swimming, and Western riding lessons, through the YMCA. She wanted to continue riding lessons but couldn't find any Western lessons. She heard about Ponca and decided to try English. "I started riding and wasn't very good," Pat laughed. "I had reached a medium level as a swimmer and tennis player, but riding was much harder. By the time I was a medium rider, I had fallen in love with horses."

She took weekly lessons for a year and then purchased her first horse, Jenny Jones, a school horse, from Glenn Cudmore. Pat, like a lot of Ponca's boarders through the years, learned about horses both from lessons and from experience. She put Jenny Jones in the cross ties, intending to use the horse vacuum in grooming. She didn't know horses need to get used to such things. She turned the vacuum on and turned around to see the halter still in the cross ties and the horse nowhere to be seen! Her next horse, a 3-year-old thoroughbred, was green but totally used to vacuums!

Sue Hull took lessons at Ponca in 1977. She remembers the Cudmores, who later ran their own barn in Crescent, Iowa. She served as DC of Ponca Pony Club for many years starting in 2001 and remains active today.

One former boarder posted on Facebook: "I loved riding at Ponca Hills in the early 70's-- so many memories-- the Cudmores, Dr. Smalley, Sue Martin, Sue Gidney, Julie Martin, pony club, a cross-country course that was amazing, Karen Mooring, Ned Tennis, --- Wonderful Place!! Thank you, Thank you."

Figure 57. Ned Tennis was a popular Ponca farm manager who originally came from Canada with the Cudmore Family.

Ned Tennis replaced Cudmore as farm manager. He came with the Cudmores from Canada to handle farming operations. At one point someone turned him in as an illegal immigrant. Allan's attorneys spent several years looking into the issue and eventually learned Ned was born in Oklahoma and adopted. Ned was very popular. One night he accompanied a group to Lashara, a small-town bar with sing-along and dancing to polka music. "Ned was a dancing energy machine," Jan recalls. "He tapped Mrs. Cudahy (Tina) to break in but then, danced away with her husband, Tony, leaving Tina surprised and sobbing with laughter on the floor."

Ned lived in a house trailer which he loved. He told Allan his goals were "to have a new suit, his own horse, a new pair of cowboy boots, a cowboy hat and a pickup. He acquired a white pickup and an old Cadillac de Ville, both of which he would loan to anyone in need," according to Jan. Since he was also a Canadian citizen, he had to

Figure 58. Pat Tschetter, Jan Moriarty, and Gary Hartnett put mare and foal into the front pasture while terrier Scooter supervises. Allan decided to raise sport horses rather than race horses.

occasionally return to Canada so he asked Dan McGuire, a farm hand, to be assistant manager.

In the mid-70s, Allen decided to go into racing as an owner and breeder and went to Kentucky, to buy "three or four" mares-in-foal. He brought 15 mares back to Ponca. Ponca Hills Farm did not have enough fenced pasture to accommodate the new arrivals, so several pastures were fenced on Ponca's hilltop meadows. When he realized what a long shot it was to breed a winning racehorse, Allan turned to breeding sport horses to have something suitable for him to ride. For several years, boarders and visitors to the farm were delighted to meet the new foals each spring, watching them cavort in the Ponca fields, and following their racing destinies.

Allan wanted to fence more pastures, and in 1979 hired Dan McGuire to help build them. "When I first started working at Ponca, there were few fenced pastures," McGuire said. "I had grown up on a farm, so I'd helped build a lot of fences; but, it's a two-man job. My

Figure 59. The Ponca "Team" ready to go fox hunting. From left, Jack Mosley and Smokey, Brad Gayman on Dakota, Allan Mactier on Saint, Mick Moriarty on Moose, and Pat Tschetter on Sophie.

father had been laid off his job, so Allan hired him to help me." The father and son built all the three rail fences at Ponca Hills Farm in 1981-1982. They rebuilt them six years later. The fences are still standing after 35 years!

McGuire took over as full-time manager after Tennis left in 1984 and continued as manager until 1989. After that he continued to work for Ponca doing fence repairs and other maintenance work for the Mactier family until present day.

Figure 60. Sue Martin Wild and Gary Harnett enjoy the sun. Sue was a rider, trainer, and instructor and all-around helper at Ponca for close to 50 years. Gary served as farm hand and then manager of the farm for 26 years.

Steve Goodrich was farm manager briefly starting in 1989 when McGuire left. Judy Csejthey managed Ponca for a few years until another farm hand, Gary Harnett, took over as farm manager in 1991. Gary had worked at Ponca for over 26 years before he retired in 2017, turning over the management job of farm and stables to his son, Jesse Harnett, who had literally grown up at Ponca.

Figure 61. Lenora Herd, barn manager, with Skye. She loves the horses and dogs and they love her.

Lenora Herd became manager of Ponca Hills Farm in 2018. She kept her horse Skye, and then her new horse River at Ponca and loves to ride out on the trails. You might be able to guess from the names of her animals, she loves Omaha's North Hills, and in particular, Ponca. She is committed to getting horses out in pastures as much as possible and maintains a clean barn and great staff of farm hands, all with a big smile. She is known for her beautiful pictures of Ponca boarders, instructors, and horses and is a smiling dynamite force mowing the many lawns around the barn.

Celebrations

Ponca Hills Farm was the scene of several engagement parties and memorable weddings. Robyn Carmichael started taking lessons and boarding at Ponca in 1970. She and Jack Eden were among the first to get married at the farm, where, by that time, they kept their four horses. They were married May 15, 1976 in a mowed field in the apple orchard on the southwest part of the property. Their reception featured a pig that had roasted all night in the farm's Hitchcock pen. The Edens still live in the North Hills where they board several horses and Robyn is an active horse show judge and steward.

Tom Ordway, a former manager and trainer at Ponca, met A rated Pony Club member Debbie McKinnon at the New Year's party at the Mactiers in 1969, the first day he had arrived at Ponca. and reconnected on his frequent trips back. They were married at the John and Jewell Grasmick farm in Seward, NE in 1981.

Jim Urban established his Northern Hills English Riding Academy at Ponca in the 80s. He met his wife Patrice at Ponca where she had, as a Creighton University student, come to take lessons. They married in 1982. Other weddings included Sam Lonigan and Billie Thone, Ethel Fletcher, and Sue Madison. Mary Ryan and Whitney Ferer met at a Ponca summer camp in 1966 and married in 1987, 21 years later. Lisa Yanney and Bill Roskens celebrated their engagement with a party at Ponca.

Happy Holidays

Figure 62. Sam Lonigan and Billie Thone both worked at Ponca and were married there. Their Christmas card pictured them on Sparrow and Miss Margaret.

Figure 63. Ponca colors, horse-drawn carriages and a Gaelic wedding united Jan Mactier and Mick Moriarty. The Wedding site is still visible as the posts remain in place, and still offers a view of downtown Omaha in the distance.

The most memorable wedding was the marriage of Jan to Mick Moriarty, September 19, 1987. The wedding had a Gaelic theme which included bagpipes, carriages, and Chip Davis' music coming from speakers in the trees. People dressed in Ponca colors. The bride rode to the wedding site in a horse-drawn carriage. Vows were exchanged on top of a hill with a view of downtown Omaha. The family, children and students came to the wedding and their parents and everyone else came to the reception, Jan said.

Figure 64. Mick and Jan Moriarty with children. Mac is on Latigo and Sheila on Miss Margaret. First blue ribbons for the kids in lead line class at North Hills Hunt Show.

A twilight reception under a voluminous white tent was illuminated by sparkling lights. As night fell and fireflies came out, the entire area was lit up by a huge fireworks display, orchestrated by Mr. Grey, who lived near the Forgot Store. Grey was the fireworks coordinator for Ak-Sar-Ben, so he included frames of cowboys, stagecoaches, and other scenes. It was a truly magical event in a magical place.

Figure 65. Jan takes "Grandma Dick," Carrie Clark Dickinson (97), and young Allan Mactier "Mac" Moriarty (10 months) on a drive with very reliable Latigo, the driving horse. Grandma Dick is holding a bunch of Sumac, thinking it a beautiful color.

More Wonderful Memories 1975 - 1995

Margie Hoffmaster started boarding her horse at Ponca in 1987. She took lessons with Jan Mactier. Sally Queal and Jim Urban were also teaching at the time. Margie often rode with Karen Theisen and Charlotte Schenken and participated in clinics with George Schneider and Karen Healey. She remembers the pony club was going strong. Like many of the riders at Ponca, they enjoyed going out on a trail and even down to the river. She tells this story:

"Anne Dolan took Anne Fortune and me on a picnic to the Missouri River. We put our lunches in Anne's saddle bags and off we went. At the river we found a nice place for lunch and hopped off our horses, tying them to a tree only to find out that Nokomis (Anne

Fortune's horse) was afraid to be tied. He took off with Anne in hot pursuit on foot. Anne Dolan jumped in her saddle and galloped Lee after them, leaving me with my horse frantic, not wanting to be left. Singing Sam was a tall thin thoroughbred and I couldn't get on. I finally found a downed tree to climb on and quickly mounted.

"I rode for about a mile and finally found my companions. One was on one side of a wire fence and one on another. As we discussed how to remedy this situation (I wasn't getting off my horse again) Clare Duda came to our rescue. We were on his property and he had been watching from a window at his home. I am sure it was very amusing to him. He offered Anne Fortune a leg up on her horse (of course she raised the wrong leg and he lifted her until discovering the error) and opened a gate so that we were reunited. We were three tired ladies and three tired horses when we got back to Ponca. We promised each other to never tell Jan this story as we knew we would have been in trouble."

Karen Theisen loved horses and started riding at Ponca in the 70s. When her daughters Amber and Crystal took lessons at Ponca and then started riding competitively in shows, Theisens had eight horses at Ponca including Lustre, Toasti, Danny Boy, Jasmine, Lickity Split, Cinnabar and Panda.

Elizabeth Hoffmaster Gregson, Margie's daughter, sent us a story of her naughty pony. "My first pony was named Celia. Her actual name was Sepia, which described her coloring perfectly, but Jan misheard the name and Celia stuck. She was adorable with a white star and three white socks. Her ears were a touch too big and her legs a touch too small. Under those perfect pony proportions, she was a tough little mare that seemed to have every bad habit in the book. She bit, kicked, bucked, stopped at fences, ran away and seemed to refuse all rider direction. Her personality was enormous and even after all of her ill behavior she is still my favorite!

"Everyone knows the trails are one of the most special things about Ponca Hills Farm. Even to this day when I find myself in an uncomfortable position in a dental chair, or in an unbearable line at the Department of Motor Vehicles, or a sleepless night of worry, I go to a certain beloved trail at Ponca which is my happy place in life.

"But before it was my happy place, the trail acted as a sort of walk of shame between Celia and me. On many occasions I would take Celia on a trail ride with my mom or other barn friends. Celia would be a perfect lady during the first half of the trail, leisurely walking (not even sneaking a bit of grass!). Everyone knew trouble was brewing just when we got to the farthest point from the barn. Celia would turn into a wild pony. She would rear, buck, shy to right, shy to the left, flat out run then stop short and end with a twirl. She did whatever it took to get me off her back and get herself home quickly to an awaiting dinner.

"Many a time the barn help would find Celia fully bridled and saddled in her stall casually munching with the door wide open. At this point a search party was sent out to find me walking home. This happened countless times until it stopped. It stopped when I stayed on that twirling pony. Years later after countless horses, I got a chance to ride her again. She was docile and sweet. I even needed spurs! She had done her job and she was satisfied. As first ponies go, Celia was the best!"

In another Missouri River ride adventure, Van Ketzler, Vicki Krecek and Kristi Wright stopped along the Missouri for a lunch. They let the horses graze while they sipped wine with sandwiches. The tranquility ended when gun shots went off across the river. The three horses, startled and took off, jumping over downed logs and headed north toward home. Vicki ran down the trail and Kristi ran along the lower level on the bank.

As Vicki passed a group of hikers, she asked if they had seen the horses. "Yes, they were beautiful," came the answer. The horses got trapped at Ponca Creek and Kristi caught Mesa, her Quarter Horse, but Patch, Vicki's horse, ran back and turned west on the trail to head home at a full gallop. Vicki said, "He'll be back." She caught Van's horse, Fox, and as they walked back to the picnic site, Patch beat them there. He always insisted on leading the herd. So much for horses contented to just graze untied!

North Hills Hunt often started its season with cubbing hunts at Ponca in the early 90s. On one ride Pat Tschetter was riding her lanky grey Appendix Quarter Horse mare Sophie. Coming up a small hill by the old farmstead just down the hill from the outdoor arena, Sophie's hind leg went into a deep hole. Pat stepped off easily as the hole buried the leg up to the crotch and Sophie, with three feet up, jumped out easily. About five other riders got off to see if they could cover or mark the hole. They spotted a pile of full-sized telephone poles and rolled one over to put in the hole. There was a collective gasp as the telephone pole sank until it only left about four feet showing above ground! It probably was an old well at the farmstead. The pole is still there, a warning to today's riders that the former uses of the land can be revealed in dangerous obstacles to riders and horses.

Figure 66. General Jack Chain, Commander, Strategic Air Command in Omaha, and Allan Mactier at a formal North Hills Hunt Ball at Offutt AFB. Music was by the SAC Band Orchestra.

General Jack Chain, a four-star general who headed the Strategic Air Command in Omaha, and his wife Judy loved to come to Ponca to ride and fox hunt with Allan. Judy would ride Teddy, a liver chestnut Morgan, out with some of the women who boarded at Ponca while Jack would go out with Allan. The Chains would show up in what the boarders called the "Bat Mobile," with the driver in charge of the communications equipment for America's air defenses. Pat Rothe remembers when Jack Chain rode in the Ponca hills, SAC would have a plane overhead to keep him in radio contact. Judy Chain always insisted on finishing her ride before Jack as she didn't want to be left.

"One winter Sunday," Vicki Krecek remembers, "Our group returned to the barn and put away our horses. It was far past the time Jack and Allan were to return but there was no sign of them. When they rode up, Jack's face was white. He was definitely in pain. Allan explained he was in the lead, galloping along in a soybean field, when

Jack's mount passed him without Jack. Allan looked back to see Jack on the ground, his radio out, calling in his position."

Figure 67. Allan, right, frequently hosted General Jack Chain and his wife Judy for a day of riding. Here they are pictured ready for fox hunting.

It turned out Jack had broken three ribs. The Base doctor told him to sleep in a recliner and said it would take about six weeks to heal, Jack replied, "You've got three days." Judy told her riding companions, "Jack has always lived on the edge."

Another time, General Chain's "Batmobile" and driver were parked at Ponca waiting for Jack to return from a ride. Just then two horses being led to the barn bolted and took off up the drive towards the entrance. Anne Dolan, a boarder, jumped in the front seat of the General's car and yelled: "Follow those horses!" The surprised driver did, and the horses were caught without further incident!

Anne Dolan and Vicki Krecek would often ride north of Ponca in the hills that backed up to Fontenelle Forest's Neale Woods. These were beautiful hills and valleys and crossed many beautiful properties, including Jungle Acres, a Christmas tree farm just northeast of Ponca. Another Hunt member, Louise Miller Gollan, said she was looking for a place in the Ponca Hills. Vicki mentioned that Jungle Acres was for sale. Louise and her husband bought the property and built a beautiful house and farm.

When they moved to Virginia, the property was purchased by Mike and Nancy McCarthy, also lovers of horses and the outdoors, who continue to maintain and expand trails on the north side of Ponca.

Figure 68. Dressed up Western style for River City Roundup are from left, Anne Dolan, Linda Gordman, and Vicki Krecek.

Linda Gordman rode Sweet Caroline at Ponca for many years. She joined Anne Dolan, on Pat, who primarily rode in a Western saddle; and Vicki, on Patch, to participate in River City Roundup parades and trail rides. Linda's brother, Larry Kavich, rode a big palomino paint, Butterscotch. Larry loved to hide carrot pieces all over Butterscotch's stall, to give him something to do when Larry was not there.

Larry Kavich's second horse was also a palomino, Rodeo, who liked to share donuts with Larry. One night after boarder, rider and stable helper Andrea Hutchinson had ridden Rodeo and put him back in the stall, she called Jan and said, "I just found a hand grenade in Rodeo's stall." Jan asked, "How do you know it's a hand grenade?" Andrea read the words and numbers on it. Jan headed straight to the barn. It was a hand grenade. She called Joe Naylon who called the sheriff. The bomb squad arrived and took it outside. It turned out to be a grenade used in military training. It could explode with noise and smoke but not blow up anything. Rodeo's stall was on the south end of the east barn and speculation was someone had tossed it in a window. Did Larry have any enemies? The mystery was solved when they learned the hay was baled in Yutan in a field the National Guard Reserves sometimes used for training. Somehow the grenade was left behind and then baled into the hay. When Rodeo ate his hay, the grenade was left on the floor.

Figure 69. Larry Kavich on Rodeo. Larry loved to ride all over the hills at Ponca and down to the River. He said these "were the best years of my life."

Larry, who passed away this summer, said he had wonderful memories of smelling snow, the first breeze of spring. "I could write a book. I'd call it The Best Years of My Life…At Ponca, of course."

Linda Gordman remembers other boarders including Gretchen Giltner, Pat Rothe, Charlotte Schenken, Tam Falvo, Jean Murphy, Linda Bezdicek (who made a career in dressage), Darlene Fellman, Nancy Gordon, Jane Kasner, Mary Jessen, Margie Hoffmaster and Mike and Fran Blose. After she retired Sweet Caroline, Linda rode Jake.

Susie Gordon Matheson said: "My grandfather, Howard Westering, gave me riding lessons at Ponca Hills Equestrian Center for my birthday when I was 10 years old. I was the only one in my family that loved horses, so my grandfather took it upon himself to get me on a horse. Allan Mactier and my grandfather had been best friends since kindergarten. I remember meeting Allan and Jan that day and Jan taking me under her wing. I was intimidated by Jan but I was determined to work hard and learn everything I could from her.

"Today," Susie continued, "I can say that Jan made the most significant impact on my life second to my family. I love Jan, I wanted her to be proud of me, I admired her. I really think that if you can find a mentor and someone you admire, and you can strive to achieve things because of that person. It will define your life. I hope that I can be that person to someone. I am forever grateful."

Susie added, "I could not get enough of the barn. It was a sacred place for me - a place of my own - my community of all ages and all types. I loved them all." She has fond memories of "the indoor ring, the smell of horses, the office, Jan's wedding site, clean tack, shirts tucked in and hair tied back, rules for life, and the rings. Someday I want to come back and ride in that front ring." And of course, Susie remembers her horses: "Acid Test-my first horse ever and my best friend and Mt. McKinley, my show horse."

Jean Murphy Rude boarded at Ponca from 1994 to 2000, when she moved to Texas with her off-the-track Thoroughbred, "No More School." She hunted with the North Hills Hunt and Gamble Hills Hounds, showed and evented and hacked at Ponca. Linda McLaren, a trainer from William Woods, was the chief trainer and manager when she first came to Ponca. Jean participated in numerous clinics with Karen Healey. and Archie Cox. "I went on several Dr. Zhivago rides, including the last one led by Mr. Mactier. Larry Kavich and Susan MacQuiddy were frequent trail buddies, and I often went out alone on the beautifully manicured trails, as my Schooley was a super trail horse. Miss it very much," she said.

Linda Gordman shared a November 18, 2003 letter from a dog Oscar, who was left behind at Ponca in 1996 by trainer Stacy Diaz. Adopted as a barn dog, Oscar developed knee issues that required major surgery. The letter from Oscar asked for donations to help with the cost of the surgery, $750, to "reconstruct what is torn in my leg." Oscar's letter to boarders continued:

"That's the bad news. The good news is my hip dysphasia is not as bad as feared and it looks like I have some miles left before I go to my final resting place. Having lived paw to mouth my entire life, I am embarrassed to say I am broke. Amy, my dear friend, has assured me her complete attention as my nurse during my healing process. Josh will allow me to stay with him in the yellow house until I am completely well, and then, we will see if I have limited access to golf cart chasing and playing fetch." Oscar concluded his letter with a plea for help and "God bless Ponca Hills Farm."

Ponca Hills Farm has always had barn dogs who get more than their share of loving from both staff and boarders. Here are a few.

Figure 70. Oscar

Figure 71. Skittles

Figure 72. From left, Ponca dogs Joy, Scooter, Biscuit, and Whisper waiting for Santa.

Figure 73. Rosie considers herself queen of Ponca and of the Hill.

Figure 74.Jan and Mick's terriers love the snow and a run in the freshly hayed fields.

Figure 75. Fathie grew to a ripe old age, nursed along by the care of many.

Fire and Ice

Figure 76. Connemara Pony Sparrow pulls the sleigh. This little mare has taught hundreds of kids on their first ever rides and is the mother of school ponies Birdie and Lamb Chop. All three horses love kids and love to jump.

Fire at Ponca

Fire! It's the very worst thing that can happen at a horse barn and it happened at Ponca Hills Farm. Brad Gayman, trainer and assistant manager, was still at the barn, setting the security alarm before leaving, when he saw smoke coming through the ceiling. He quickly dialed 911 and then called Mick and Jan who were just sitting down to dinner with Jack Mosley. Mick and Jack headed up the hill to the barn.

It was November 8, 1991 and the temperature was less than 5 degrees. It was a week after a Halloween blizzard left two inches of ice covering the barn roof. The smoke was coming from the east barn where the fire, started by a malfunction in the large heater, was burning in the wooden rafters.

Brad began leading horses into the large attached indoor arena. He figured that once there, they could be pushed out through the huge doors if that part of the barn caught fire. He didn't want to push the horses into the ice-covered paddocks outside unless it became necessary. Brad was soon joined by Mick and Jack.

The smoke was quickly filling the barn. The ceiling was on fire and collapsing under the weight of the ice. Brad, Mick and Jack were finding horses in their stalls by feel, because they couldn't see them in the thick smoke. They led them to the indoor arena, brushing embers from their jackets as they went.

Clare Duda, Ponca Volunteer Fire Department Chief, had just finished dinner at his farm along the river just north of Dodge Park when the call came in. He and the other Ponca volunteer firefighters dashed to the station, which is less than a mile from Ponca Hills Farm. Twenty of Ponca's 35 volunteer firefighters responded, and they got to the barn in record time.

As they arrived, Duda said his heart was pounding, "The smoke and flames were stubborn, and there was a false report that someone was still in the building." There was panic when no one could find Mick in the thick smoke and worried that he was still in the barn.

"Horse barns are scary things," Duda told the World-Herald a week after the fire. "Their size and construction and all the wood make them difficult. The size of this barn is awesome, and there's no good water source nearby."

Ponca's barn sits at the top of a hill and, since the area has no bedrock, Ponca's wells went down 300 or more feet. That meant there was little water pressure - not enough to fight a fire. It required water tank trucks. In all, ten tanker-loads of water, 1,000 gallons each, were hauled in to fight the fire.

Jan was at home with two-year-old Mac and her infant daughter, Sheila. "Mac and I stood in the window and watched fire truck after truck race up the hill, then back, going many places to fill up with water," Jan said. "We were frightened not knowing what was happening. Word went out over the radio and people came from everywhere to help."

Because it was a fire in a building, volunteer fire departments from Fort Calhoun and Irvington also responded, bringing over 60 firefighters and many engines to the scene. The Boys Town Volunteer Fire Department immediately came in as back up, standing by at the Ponca station in case of another fire. At the same time, Elkhorn volunteers moved into the Irvington station and the Blair volunteers covered the Fort Calhoun station.

They accomplished a miracle. The firemen were able to put out the fire with only damage to the east barn. All horses from stalls in that wing were evacuated to the arena. It was an almost unheard-of victory in a barn fire. Most barn fires are a total loss, including the livestock! Firemen said five more minutes and the barn would have been lost.

Why was this fire successfully put out? Ponca Hill's volunteer fire department had visited Ponca Hills Farm just two weeks before as a part of their fire preparedness training. "It's the largest building and concern in our fire district," Duda later told the Omaha World-Herald. "We had done a lot of pre-planning on it."

All boarders were called by 9:30 to let them know there had been a fire, and their horses were safe. There was also relief that horses did not need to be turned out on the icy hills surrounding the arena. Chief Duda arrived home at 1 a.m.

How could so many grateful horse owners possibly thank these great volunteer fire fighters? One boarder was Larry Caniglia whose parents owned the Omaha landmark restaurant Mister Cs. Larry, Larry Kavich, Anne Dolan, and others organized a big dinner party for all the firefighters, their families and the Ponca staff and boarders at Mister Cs. It was a heartfelt celebration, paid for by the boarders and Mactiers. Over 140 people attended. It was an evening of celebration for all.

That gratitude continues. The firefighters do their work without pay and the department is funded by tax dollars and fund raising. Today, 30 years later, Ponca Hills Farm boarders and staff join the Ponca Hills community in continuing to support fund-raising spaghetti feeds, barbecues and pancake feeds at the Ponca Hills Volunteer Fire Department.

The Omaha World-Herald, revisiting the barn two weeks after the fire, reported: "Late last week, at the highest point in the hills, the barn ceiling was still charred, but the place was busy. Cats scurried about, and a Dalmatian barked. Horses occasionally whinnied. Up and down the stable row, horses named Spats, Rebate, Linus, Bubba and Sweet Caroline looked just fine." The ceiling and roof of the east barn were rebuilt quickly.

On another occasion a spark from the manure dump blew and caught the newly filled hay barn, which at that time was located where the machine shed and trailers are parked today. Jan remembers many firetrucks as the fire smoldered and restarted for a long time. The barn was a total loss. Insurance covered the barn, but not the contents. The hay barn was moved to the present location, a long way from the barn.

Figure 77. Rick Eckhardt, manager and instructor in the mid 70s attempts to lighten the snow load on the indoor arena.

Snow and Ice

In Nebraska, weather is an ever-present concern, especially for a farm with livestock. Jan Moriarty remembers many winter horse shows and other events affected by extreme weather. Extreme snow, ice, rain, and wind are frequent challenges in the hilly country. Several times 42nd street, the only access to the farm, was closed due to snow drifts. Horses in stalls need a steady supply of hay and water.

When storms result in no electricity, the pumps can't run. It takes several days for Ponca's cisterns to run dry. Once the cisterns ran dry and water was brought in from Jan's house and the Ponca Volunteer Fire Barn to fill tanks and buckets to water horses throughout the day. Today the farm is still on well water, but the houses along Hawk Wood Circle now have replaced well water with NRD water.

Ponca hosted a Hans Senn clinic one winter. Jan remembers: "There was a big blizzard. The snow was totally drifted over 42nd street before Snow Drift Road. The guys at the barn decided they would rather be snowed in at my parents' home, so they were. They would hike back and forth. The house was full of people playing pool and playing the album 'Jesus Christ Superstar' over and over and over. There was lots of noise - even chaos. When the roads and airport were finally open, Hans, a Swiss bachelor, snowbound for three or four days, fled to the airport."

She also recalls a major winter storm: "When Dad brought 15 broodmares who were in foal from Kentucky in the 80s, Elmer Jespersen convinced the Douglas County sand trucks to sand the road from the Interstate, along with 47th Street, Ponca Road, 42nd Street, our driveway, and from the horse truck to the West Barn door. It was solid ice the whole way. Fortunately, all arrived safely."

An Archie Cox clinic was scheduled during one Blizzard. All the jumps were in the hay barn and the road from the horse barn to the hay barn was totally drifted closed. Tractors and plows were all stuck. Jan recalled that the barn hands went to sleep in the office because they couldn't leave. "The next morning, they went through the field on foot and saved the day by bringing in the jumps. They gave up on plowing because all the tractors were stuck in snowdrifts."

There was another tremendous snowstorm in late October 1997. The wet snow snapped tree limbs, still heavy with fall foliage, sounding like rifle fire. Limbs and trees split, buckled and fell to the ground, taking power lines with them. Up to two feet of snow left hundreds of thousands of people across the metro area without power, some for a week or more. That Sunday morning recorded a record 9.2 inches of snow and ice.

Most of the roads into the Ponca Hills area were completely cut off by white walls of trees. It was a fairy land to look at, but Ponca's beautiful trails were a war zone. Even its widest trails were cut off by large trees and limbs.

At the barn, the crew was kept busy bringing buckets of water to horses as power had shut off the automatic waterers. They worked tirelessly plowing open roads to the barn and hay barn. The last thing on their priority list was the clearing of Ponca's beautiful trails.

The weekend after the storm, a crew of about fifteen volunteers showed up with chainsaws and clippers. Among them were several members of the North Hills Hunt including Vicki and Dave Krecek and son John, Susan MacQuiddy and Jon Shepherd, Van Ketzler, and Ron Dudley. Although none boarded at Ponca at the time, they all enjoyed coming to hunt events at Ponca and so joined in to clear trails. While working on trails, Susan MacQuiddy learned Ron Dudley's house on River Road was for sale. She bought the house and shortly after moved her horse Oliver to Ponca Hills Farm, where Oliver is still happy in retirement today.

Wind and Rain

Ponca has seen many tornadoes and almost tornadoes, winds, wall clouds, circular telescoping clouds, Mediterranean blue skies as well as ghastly green and yellow skies. It has experienced blasts of hot and cold air, lightning from horizon to horizon, large hail and lots of thunderstorms. Jan Moriarty laughed, "Gretchen Hennecke's hair would stick straight up with the lightning."

During several of Karen Healey's clinics, it rained torrentially, 4, 6, 10 inches in 24 hours. Ponca Hills Farm, standing atop Omaha's highest hill, misses the flooding from such heavy downpours, but it was worse for those trailering in. The Interstate to Des Moines was closed. People coming to clinic had to take back roads.

Figure 78. Storms come in fast and are spectacular from Ponca. A major tower marks the highest point (except for Phil's Hill) in Omaha in the "Tower Pasture."

There was also drought. Jan remembers, "During drought we would water the outdoor ring by hand for the Karen Healey clinics."

On June 5, 2014, Nancy Gardner of the Omaha World-Herald reported:

"Northeast Nebraska was the site of an intense hailstorm Tuesday, with images of damage quickly going viral. The damage was a reflection of the intense power of the storm. In several communities, the hail was the size of baseballs, including in Norfolk, Blair and Fort

Calhoun. The largest hailstone in eastern Nebraska was reported near Kennard — 4.25 inches in diameter. Wind speeds reached 91 mph near Kennard to 100 mph at Newport.

"Imagine being in Fort Calhoun and Blair as hail as big as baseballs pelted homes at speeds of 80 to 91 mph. According to the National Weather Service, hailstones in the two communities measured 2.75 inches across. The nearest wind sensors — at Fort Calhoun Nuclear Station and Kennard — measured peak speeds at 80 mph and 91 mph, respectively. Lt. Aaron Barrow of the Blair Police Department said the hailstorm sounded like a 'million hammers' striking the side of the cinder-block police station."

Jan Moriarty was in Samur, France at FEI International Driving Competition getting ready for WEG at Normandy. Team USA won the Bronze Medal. "Fortunately, my own video changed our elimination to 'clear,' resulting in the USA getting the Bronze Medal," Jan said. But good news was followed by bad. "I got several phone calls about a big storm at home. Ten windows were broken at my house plus roof, siding, paint, etc. Three sides of the house had to be replaced."

The barn suffered over $800,000 in damages including broken windows and skylights, damage to the roof and three sides. The bad news was all the reconstruction of barn and outbuildings had just been finished. The good news was the construction crew was still on site. So, they rebuilt it again: roofs, windows, siding.....much of it not a year old. It took several years to rebuild again. "Too Bad the Hail Storm didn't come one year earlier," Jan mused. "It would have saved a lot of money.

Ponca Hills Farm Today

Legacy of the Land - The Ponca Preserve

Figure 79. Allan Mactier leads a group of riders over a roll top jump on the cross-country course. His eye for natural beauty guided the building of trails and cross-country courses to assure a beautiful ride in any season.

Besides the dedication to education of riders, the Mactier family has a history of commitment to be good stewards of the land. The forest includes White Oak, Bur Oak, Pin Oak, Red Oak, native Ash, Elm, Ohio Buckeye, Hickory, Hackberry, Kentucky Coffee, Sycamore, Cottonwood, Willow, Wild Plum, Linden, Silver Maple, and Black Walnut trees, as well as hundreds of varieties of bushes and grasses.

"Dad loved trees," daughter Jan said. "Every day was a good day to plant a tree. He often took trees from the woods and planted them elsewhere." He added evergreens and flowering crabs to the areas framing the farm. Allan planted so many evergreens around the farm because they are fast growing trees.

Figure 80. "Phil's Hill" is the highest point in Omaha. Mary Celer and Tipper enjoy the view, perhaps thinking about the many Pony Club riders who took this jump at the National Rally in 1973.

The Loess Hills, on which the barn is located, has no bedrock as the hills were originally formed from topsoil blown in. As a result, erosion is a constant problem and owner Jan Moriarty maintains an ongoing program of preserving these hills and stopping erosion. Starting in 2000, Jan has increased pasture acreage and reduced the steep drops to the ravine behind the barn and yellow house and also towards the wedding site. Truckloads of dirt were used to level and fill eroded slopes, creating pastures for hay. A new machine shed was built and gravel was added to several farm roads.

The nature-preserve trails have also undergone major improvements and conservation efforts led by Mick Moriarty. Mick enlists the help of students and others in refurbishing cross-country jumps, building new obstacles, controlling erosion, maintaining native plants, and building new and challenging trails.

Because of Mick, fallen trees are removed from trails, bushes cut back when they block trails, and paths and jump approaches are beautifully mowed. Maintaining miles of trails through woods and across meadows is a constant job which can only be fully appreciated if you have tried to ride off trail in a wet summer!

Figure 81. Dutchmen's Breeches are the first to bloom in spring forest.

A hack through the Ponca trails in any season provides a show of wildflowers and wildlife. The well-kept trails through the woods offer a variety of jumps over logs and log-built jumps. Mick is always excited to introduce riders to his new trails, some of which drop precipitously into ravines or offer a new route through the woods. He spends considerable time grooming trails preparing to welcome The North Hills Hunt, Competitive Trail Ride and local saddle clubs to Ponca Hills Farm for clinics, rides and events.

Riders who take to the trails at Ponca get a year-round, constantly changing course in the natural environment, hills and forests, just 20 minutes from downtown Omaha. Riders can see the high-rise buildings of downtown Omaha from the wedding site of Mick and Jan, from the Tower pasture, from the Phil's Hill, and from the northeast pastures. Then quickly they can drop down to ravines lush with native vegetation.

First in the spring is a tiny hint of green, quickly followed by the delicate Dutchman's Breeches. A few days later blue violets blossom amid the unfolding tiny fiddle ferns. Next come Wild Blue Phlox snuggled among the (from the horse's perspective) oh-so-yummy grasses and then Sweet William. In the spring riders can easily ride off trail on a "freelance" exploration of the woods without nettles.

As summer approaches and the ground cover thickens, riders take a more hospitable route along the wide, beautifully laid out trails first envisioned by Allan Mactier and Philip Durbrow, and largely built by Elmer Jespersen. Durbrow remembers being with Allan and Elmer on his bulldozer inside the rollover cage. Elmer would hold up his hand stop and open the operating manual, saying, "There are no directions in here to do what we are doing." Elmer was an artist with a bulldozer, according to Jan.

Figure 82. Ponca Hills Farm sits atop of the highest point in Omaha, surrounded by pastures, and forests on the hills near the Missouri River. Photo taken in fall 1990.

As a result of their efforts, there are plenty of hills to challenge horse and rider. Trails meander along the steep banks beside Thomas Creek and the heavy forest provides cool shade in summer and protection from the wind. The careful planning created a lasting treat for trail riders.

The fall is spectacular in the woods. First the Sumac turns deep red. Next the wide variety of trees provide a daily changing color, from new green, to yellow, to deep red. When most of the colorful leaves have fallen, one bank of the ravine just past Ponca's northern boundary turns into fairy land. Wild Burning Bush puts out a watercolor salmon-colored tableau against the now brown forest. One young rider exclaimed, "It looks just like Japan!" The trails are covered with fallen leaves, but the horses know the way, so a loose rein will be all you need to stay on course. After the first hard frost, it is once again possible to explore many different parts of the wooded areas by riding off trail.

Figure 83. Wild Burning Bush puts out a watercolor salmon-colored tableau against the now brown forest. One young rider exclaimed, "It looks just like Japan!"

But the ultimate view is when every tree branch is covered with a thick blanket of new snow. Horses trotting through the deep snow placing their riders into a living Christmas card! Jan pulls out her sleigh and hitches it to one of her ponies. Mick gets out his cross-country skis, and horses snort at the newly transformed world. This is when you know that Ponca Hills Farm really is Camelot!

Figure 84. Riders head out to the north pastures in a new snowfall.

Deer are plentiful all over the Ponca Preserve and aren't that alarmed by people on horses. They turn a beautiful grey in winter with black outlining their ears. In summer, little fawns are more curious than scared. Turkeys are abundant and funny as they hurry off the trail or awkwardly fly to a tree branch or hustle their little ones along. The horses are used to turkeys as they are frequent companions in their pastures, but a little more cautious when the males are in full and shaking tail with very loud gobble-gobble voices.

Owls are a little harder to spot - but they fly middle of tree to middle of another tree (or ground to middle), and you can spot them once they land. Hawks are everywhere and there are often a couple of bald eagles lazily circling above or, if you're lucky, perched in a tree right above you. The woods are full of woodpeckers, flickers, Baltimore orioles and even bluebirds.

Find a friend and take a ride around the property. You will pass some of the vestiges of the National Pony Club Rally held in 1973. The small pond on the hill northeast of the barns was designed as a water obstacle with natural log jumps at various heights in and out. It is sometimes referred to as "Blose Lake," after longtime Ponca farrier, Mike Blose, because horses tend to lose shoes in the muddy bottom. In the woods across the northeast pasture from the pond is the overgrown remains of a wooden triple jump constructed for the rally and painted with house paint from the Mactier's house. And there is

Figure 85. Riders Mike and Nancy McCarthy and neighbor Gale McKeen, head out across one of Ponca's high pastures which doubles as a cross-country course.

always the welcoming Ponca signature "Phil's Hill" in the high pasture at Ponca's entrance and the Piano Jump in the south ravine. The first cross-country jumps were built on the property behind the barn in the north valley and hills. The course was added to as the Mactiers acquired additional land.

As one cowboy put it "Sometimes gets as good as this but it don't get no better!"

146

Figure 86. Bald eagle watches riders pass underneath near the mares' pasture at Ponca.

Figure 87. Jan and Mick Moriarty gallop through the water jump originally designed for the National Pony Club Rally and still enjoyed by riders today. They are riding Ponca bred horses Fuzzy and Red Max.

A Community of Neighbors

Figure 88. Ariel eyes the lovely grass at an old homestead. The pole in center is actually a full-sized telephone pole which was used to mark a hole after a horse stepped in it. The hole turned out to be an old well which nearly swallowed the pole.

Ponca Hills Farm is a part of a neighborhood of horse people and others who love Omaha's north hills. Immediately at the bottom of the hill, east of the barn are a few remainders of a small farm. There is the telephone pole (with only four feet visible above ground) marking a deep hole, to prevent a recurrence of a horse stepping in.

Gary Young, leading a trail ride at Ponca for the Stockyards Saddle Club, said he grew up in that spot. His parents, Roy and Dorothy Young, bought 40 acres off Shongasta Road in 1958. Roy worked as a horseman, moving cattle at the Union Stockyards Company in Omaha. He founded the Stockyards Saddle Club as a way for the stockyards riders to have fun and do shows on weekends. After Roy died and Dorothy moved to town, Gary lived in the house and cared for the family's horses. He was married in 1965 and he and his wife lived there until 1971 when he sold the acreage to Allan Mactier. Dan McGuire, who worked at Ponca, lived in that farmhouse until it burned down about 1973. Young spent his school-age years living at 63rd and Center and spent much of his time across the street at Ak-Sar-Ben racetrack where he hot walked horses before going to school in the mornings. The Stockyards Saddle Club is still very active and today owns property and a riding arena on 60th, just north of Highway 36, but Gary always enjoys the groups' rides at Ponca.

Riding to the north from that old homestead, riders first pass "Blose Lake" on the right (named for all the horse shoes lost while crossing) and then on the left, Ann and Jim McGuire's acreage nestled in the hills at the head of Shongasta Road. They board a few horses there and have turned a very old farmhouse into comfortable home with beautiful antiques, a tribute to Ann's talent as a longtime graphic artist with Mutual of Omaha.

Riders then head into the woods bordering Ponca's north boundary. Today Mike and Nancy McCarthy own much of that wooded area and enjoy trail rides in the forest and generously let others ride those trails.

Neighbor Gail McKeen boards horses and leads rides and is a diligent caretaker of trails, clearing downed trees and brush, and rerouting trails which are becoming eroded. Gale, a woodworker, is also responsible for the carved wooden signs designating trail names, giving directions, and offering horse-related philosophical quotes. One sign in the northern woods read: "A canter is a cure for every evil."

Figure 89. Gale McKeen not only keeps trails open on the land just north of Ponca Hills Farm, he uses his wood working abilities to impart a little philosophy to the passing riders.

Further west along the north boundary, is a former Thoroughbred breeding and training facility owned by the family of the late Dr. McCarthy (no relation to Mike). The racehorses have been replaced by boarded horses, but remnants of the old exercise track remain. To the Northwest, Ponca adjoins the farm of Dorothy and Don Tripp. Don still raises corn and soybeans and has pastures for grazing cattle. Dorothy loves riding her palomino on the pastures and trails. She was born and grew up on that farm.

Figure 90. Allan created this pond in the mid 80s because he felt every farm should have a pond.

Between Tripp's and Ponca is a beautiful pond built by Allan purely to add beauty to the land. They built a small dam across the ravine. Karen Theisen on Panda was the first to ride across the dam in 1987. In the fall, the resulting pond is home to colorful wood ducks and in the summer offers a place to canoe. The pond is spring fed and drains into Thomas Creek. It has turned into an incredible wildlife sanctuary.

Moving south, along the west side, a ravine separates Ponca Hills Farm from the acreage owned by Jeff Ketzler and his wife Sue. Jeff is owner of the Dehner Company, maker of custom-made English riding and military boots. A former Pony Clubber and fox hunter, Jeff is a big supporter of the Ponca Hills area and cooks a large pot of black-eyed peas for the New Year's Day breakfast after the Dr. Zhivago ride.

Chip Davis, owner of American Gramophone and creator of Mannheim Steamroller, lives south of the Ketzlers. He purchased an acreage from Mactier for his home. Later he purchased the Voss farmhouse, also from Allan, for a guest house for the many musicians who travel to Omaha to work with him. Melvin Voss owned the white two-story farmhouse near the cemetery on 47th Street, on the south border of Chip's property. Allan bought the property from Voss. Chip is a huge promoter of preservation of the land and nature, incorporating nature's sounds, gathered from microphones in those woods, into his recordings.

Figure 91. The small white house was to be moved from Lisa Roskens' farm to Ponca Hills Farm and was mounted on wheels for the trip. In the night it rolled down the hill and landed across from Don and Dorothy Tripp's farm.

Lisa Yanney Roskens loved the North Hills and purchased land for a horse farm just west of Chip Davis. She built a beautiful home, barn, arenas and pasture on the former cattle ranch. There was a small white farmhouse on her land which was, for a while, rented by Lindsay Sophir, another Ponca Pony Club graduate. Lisa didn't want the house and offered it to the Mactiers to move to their farm. It was loaded onto a platform for moving, when one night it got loose and rolled down the hill, stopping across from the Tripp's, who were astonished to see a house in what had been a farm field the day before. The house stayed here for several months while the Mactier's figured out the best way to move it to Ponca. To avoid moving the numerous power lines along 47th and 42nd streets, which was very costly, they moved it through the Voss land to Ponca. This was accomplished by moving just two gate posts and a guy wire. The Mactiers built a basement and put the house on the foundation. Ann Mactier exclaimed: "It looks like it has always been there." Sophir had left a bottle of wine in the sink, which, Jan says, arrived with the house, sitting where Lindsay left it.

Figure 92. The white house was moved to Ponca and is providing a cozy home for farm hands.

Figure 93. Ponca Hills Farm is able to supply much of its hay from its own fields.

Farm Improvements Continue

After Allan's death in 2005, Jan purchased a farmhouse and 20 acres across from the entrance to Ponca. She renovated the house and carriage house and filled the house with her extensive collection of antique furniture and quilts. It provides a great place for a holiday party or housing guests. The acreage supplies hay for Ponca.

Jan and her mother felt renovations were needed to the barn. After 40 years the indoor roof and insulation needed replacing, the pipes were aging, and the bathrooms needed refurbishing. They remodeled the upstairs viewing gallery, and added insulation, heat, windows, and new staircase in the school barn. They insulated and raised floors in the trainer's and manager's offices and created a separate laundry room and enlarged and remodeled bathrooms.

In the barns, they removed all dropped ceilings and replaced lights and insulation. The entire water system and copper pipes were replaced with plastic, and they added water and insulation in the quarantine barn and new drain and pipes in the West Barn wash stall. All the pipes in the entire barn were replaced. The Middle Barn was totally rebuilt adding insulation and skylights. They rebuilt and extended the roof area to help solve water leaking into barn and added a furnace, and lockers for storage. The entire Middle Barn foundation was replaced, and they replaced windows and skylights, giving that barn more air circulation and light.

The Pony Club viewing room was rebuilt, adding insulation and a new ceiling. Cement was added outside the Pony Club Room for a patio and storage and to prevent water leaking into the room.

Cement was also added outside towards the Show Ring and Dressage Ring to facilitate drainage. A cistern and drainage were added on the hill to the outdoor show ring. A drainage cistern was also added near the back pasture.

The workshop was enlarged, and they added a new location for shavings storage. Cement was added between Hitchcock Pen and Middle Barn for better drainage.

A Special Setting for Special Events

Figure 94. Mactiers hosted many hunt breakfasts, community events, elegant dinners, and Hunt Breakfasts on the lawn. In threatening weather, in the aisles of Ponca's barn became the dining hall while horses looked on.

Both Ann and Allan were heavily involved in the community and were willing and hospitable hosts for community events. Ann remained the owner and manager of Ponca Hills Farm until 1973. Allan was active in several organizations, including serving as president of the Greater Omaha Chamber of Commerce and Ak-Sar-Ben Board of Governors. From its beginning, Ponca Hills Farm had a welcome mat out for community events.

The barn aisles have been transformed for elegant dinners, with horses looking on from their stalls. The green pastures have been scenes of picnics, concerts and fundraisers. The Chamber of Commerce has held meetings here. There have been countless charity events, including for the Nature Conservancy, Ak-Sar-Ben, Opera Omaha, HETRA, and other events. Take Flight Farms, started by Lisa Yanney Roskens as a therapy program for emotionally challenged young people, got its start at Ponca using some of the farm's horses. Allan and Ann for years invited business associates, friends, neighbors and boarders to a spring "Hunt Breakfast" on the lawn. Several hundred people enjoyed a beautiful picnic, entertained by a jumping demonstration in the front pasture, or in some years, mares frolicking with new foals.

Figure 95. A Hunt Breakfast on the lawn included (L to R) John Gaskin, Lowell Boomer, Ann Grasmick, Jewell Grasmick, and John Grasmick.

As founder of the Phoenix Academy, Ann invites its students for a field trip to the farm. In 2019, 110 students from the school came enjoy a day at Ponca, complete with hay rack rides, hikes and games.

Ann Mactier celebrated her 90th birthday on June 29, 2012. Everyone was invited - family, friends, boarders, friends of friends, the neighborhood. There were Pony Clubbers, the mayor, Opera Omaha and Omaha Symphony friends, veterinarians, and grade school friends. Family and grandchildren came from Poland. A big tent was set up at Phil's Hill in the southwest pasture at the Farm entrance. Its sides were open so guests could watch the sunset and to enjoy as much breeze as possible

(The evening was extremely hot with the temperature still at 103' at 6:00 P.M.) The humidity was about the same.) The tent was furnished with rugs, sofas, chairs, and light fixtures. It offered a photo booth, pinball, fabulous food, and glow toys for children and adults. And there was a large dance floor - and a wonderful surprise - Peter Duchin. Jan had met Duchin several times when she was horse

Figure 96. Allan Mactier greets a group gathered for the announcement of Mick and Jan's engagement.

showing in Florida. "We both stayed in Palm Beach several times at the Mahoneys because of our mutual Idaho friends Sheila and Eb Gaines," Jan explained.

The crowd danced as Peter Duchin played the piano with his band from New York. The dancing and celebrating went late into the night. The evening ended with fireworks. Jan recalls: "It was a really big show and Mom had a really good time. A favorite memory was Charlie Nielson from Shady Lane telling my Mom some tall tales. She was laughing with a look showing she was enjoying but not believing a word he said."

Figure 97. Summer campers Katie Krantz (Right) and Layla Messer working with Fella.

For over 55 years, Ponca Hills Farm has continued as a center of riding activities, hunt breakfasts, Pony Club meetings, lessons, and clinics. Ponca has sponsored riding camps for youngsters for over half a century. Summer camps are often sold out in January, and former campers, now grown, are sending their children and grandchildren for their first lessons. The format is essentially the same.

Figure 98. Madison Webb takes her first lessons on Sparrow, Ponca's number one Connemara pony.

Figure 99. When Archie Cox came to Ponca to do clinics he often conducted lessons for kids in summer camp.

Youngsters learn how to safely groom, tack up, ride out and take care of their equine charges. And like all summer camps, there is plenty of fun, including picnics, horse shows and all-around mischief. One mother wrote, "My daughter attended summer camp for the first time and absolutely cannot stop talking about it! She loved it and can't wait to go back and start taking lessons!"

Today the Ponca Hills Farm school program continues to teach students of all ages the fundamentals of correct riding. Top clinicians such as Canadian show jumper Karen Cudmore and Idaho- based hunter trainer Tom Ordway, frequently visit Ponca, drawing participants from around the region. Ponca Hills Farm Summer Camp, established by Ann Mactier in 1965, continues to offer education, riding instruction and fun to dozens of area youth every June and July.

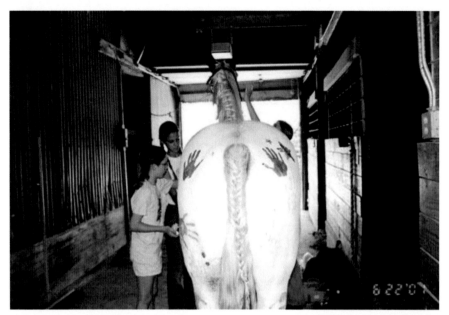

Figure 100. Decorating a white horse is always a fun activity for kids in summer camps.

Natalie Shaw, who came to Ponca for riding lessons as a youngster, pays it forward as a popular and positive instructor, setting out a challenging course of small jumps for tiny people on tiny ponies or seasoned school horses. Caleb Cooney, a young and enthusiastic professional rider/trainer, is bringing a new energy to the lessons and training programs at Ponca.

One person wrote on Ponca Hills Farm Facebook page, "This farm doesn't deserve a 5-star review, it deserves better! We came for the Tom Ordway clinic, Tom was great! He sets the bar high and I honestly don't know why there wasn't a line down the drive for the clinic! But I know why he comes, other than nostalgia: everyone at the

Figure 101. Sometimes summer camp kids learn to harness and drive a pony. Jan Moriarty says, "Because of Pat Tschetter we have driving at Ponca.

barn was so nice, super helpful. Being fairly new to the jumping circuit but 38 years old to horse shows, I can honestly say I've never met a nicer bunch of horse people ever! Not one rude look, or mean comment mumbled anywhere by anyone! I've seen the nasty side of the horse world, but it's definitely not here! I felt like I was back with my 4H club growing where everyone was equal and helped each other. I would, and will, trailer 3 hours there again without hesitation!"

Whether they come for a short time or stay for years boarding their horses here, this is a place many people feel is a home. The horse industry has changed radically as it entered the 21st century, and Ponca Hills Farm has had a lasting commitment to providing quality care for boarder horses and educational opportunities for riders, Pony Clubbers and campers. Through good times and challenging ones, Ponca Hills Farm has remained true to the values of its founders.

Figure 103. Tom Ordway comes back to Ponca several times a year to work with riders in a variety of disciplines.

Figure 102. Carine Stava takes a jump at a "Safe Rider" Clinic she holds with North Hills Hunt. Mick Moriarty, who hunts every year in Ireland, provides helpful hints for taking jumps in the hunt field.

Today, Jan Mactier Moriarty continues her parents' vision for the farm and excellence in education for correct riding and care of horses. Under Jan's guidance, since 2004, Ponca remains an active barn with boarders who both compete and ride for pleasure on Ponca's extensive trails.

Dee Hudson recently commented, "It is very obvious the deep love and respect that Jan has for Ponca Hills. She is so very proud of it and is forever continuing to improve it. Her father would be so proud of her. Thanks for all the wonderful lifelong memories."

Figure 104. Mick Moriarty drives Ann Mactier out to watch a cross-country jumping clinic (2019).

Appendix
Standards of Excellence - Rules and Wisdom

Today riders brushing horses in cross ties often wonder why Ponca has such insistence on doing things certain ways. The answer is in the history of riding as a military discipline. Military and education emphasize standards of excellence - doing things correctly. The underlying reason is safety. Ponca Rules state: "Designed for the safety of our boarders, guests, employees and horses." The military needed trained riders and obedient and willing horses. The fox hunting group helped provide both, and Pony Clubs served as feeder groups to fox hunts.

Barn Rules

- A neat stable area is a safer stable area. Keep trash picked up, tools hung up (Sharp ends facing the wall) and equipment such as wheelbarrows stored out of the way.
- Leading a horse under cross ties which hold another horse can result in a saddle catching on the cross tie and a rodeo!
- Always lead a horse with a halter and lead rope, not by holding onto the halter or a rope around the neck. It will prevent loose horses, shoulders pulled out of joint, and dangling children.
- When handling a horse, keep your attention on him and keep his attention on you. Be aware of the things that could spook him and keep a safe distance from other horses.
- When leading a horse through a gate or out of a stall, open the gate or door wide and be sure the latch is not sticking out where it could catch him.
- When turning horses loose in pasture or stall, close the gate and make them turn to face you before you let go.
- Halters should be left on so they can easily be led out in an emergency. Use a breakable leather halter.
- Cross ties should be equipped with safety strings.
- Don't leave a horse unattended when tied or cross tied.
- Unplug electrical appliances when not in use.

- Don't ride through barns.
- Hard hats are mandatory when mounted.
- Know where fire extinguishers are and how to use them.
- Remove halters attached to cross ties or from tie rope. An attached halter lying on the floor can catch in a horse's foot resulting in injury.
- Keeping saddles, bridles, feed etc. in proper places and containers can prevent wear, loss, spills.
- Stable floors should be kept clean.

Recommendations of Cavalry/Pony Club and Others

- Shirts not tucked in can flap around and catch on doors or machinery causing an injury. Tucked in clothes can help a trainer see the rider's position.
- Put saddles on saddle racks pommel first not only looks more uniform, but you can see whose saddle is whose.
- Clean tack after every ride. Wipe dust, dirt and sweat off. Condition leather as needed. Dry leather can break and is unsafe. Dirty equipment can cause sores.
- Patience with a horse will get you further faster than trying to hurry a horse.
- Pick out a horse's feet before and after each ride to remove stones and wet manure.
- Wait for the horse to relax before asking him/her to do something like walking into a trailer, or approaching a strange object or obstacle on the trail, etc.
- Rules for arena riding mean safety when there are numerous people riding. Left shoulder to left shoulder when passing on the rail. Like in boating, the one in least control has the right of way.
- Put a red ribbon in a horse's tail if it is green or a kicker can prevent a broken leg of another rider.
- Warm a horse up for at least 20 minutes before jumping, and cooling down afterwards, can help prevent injuries, future lameness or health problems.
- Military drills can teach horses and riders how to control direction and speed of the horse when riding in groups.

Ponca Pony Club District Commissioners

1967 - 32 girls, 13 boys
Ann Mactier DC

1968 - 32 girls, 13 boys
Ann Mactier DC
Gretchen Giltner, Jt DC
Mrs. A. Cudahy, Secr.

1969 - 32 girls 8 boys
Ann Mactier DC
Don Dunn Jt DC
Mrs. Anthony Cudahy,
Secretary

1970 - 56 girls 12 boys
Ann Mactier DC
Don Dunn Jt DC
Mrs. Anthony Cudahy,
Secretary

1971 - 35 girls 10 boys
Don Dunn DC
Ken Naughton Jt DC
Mrs. Anthony Cudahy,
Secretary

1972 - 35 girls, 10 boys
Ken Naughton DC
Mrs. Anthony Cudahy,
Secretary

1973 - 46 girls, 18 boys
Ken Naughton DC
Ann Mactier Jt DC

1974 - 46 girls, 13 boys
Ken Naughton DC
Ann Mactier Jt DC

1976 - 34 girls, 4 boys
Ken Naughton DC
Vem Salestrom Co DC
Dr. And Mrs. Ted Urban,
Secretary

1977
Vem Salestrom DC
Ken Naughton Jt DC

Sue Urban, Secretary
Gwen Madison,
Corresponding Secr.

1978 - 37 girls, 9 boys
Vem Salestrom DC
Ken Naughton Jt DC
Gwen Madison, Secr.

1979 - 35 girls, 8 boys
Vem Salestrom DC
Ken Naughton Jt DC
Gwen Madison, Secr.

1980 - 39 girls 11 boys
Vem Salestrom DC
Ken Naughton Jt DC
Gwen Madison, Secr.

1981
Vem Salestrom DC
Trish Lamphier Jt DC
Gwen Madison, Secr.

1982 - 27 girls 7 boys
Vem Salestrom DC
Trish Lamphier Jt DC
Merrilee Hansen, Secr.
Susie Tinstman, Tres.

1983 - 28 girls, 7 boys
Vem Salestrom DC
Gwen Madison, Secr.
Susie Tinstman, Tres.

1984 - 18 girls, 1 boy
Vem Salestrom DC
Renee Kasner, Secr.
Penny Markworth, Tres.

1985 - 30 members
Vem Salestrom DC
Sherma Seitzinger Jt DC
Salli Roberts, Tres.
Judy Irwin, Sece.

1986

Jan Redick, DC
Sharon O'Brien, Jt DC
Steve Bowman, Tres.
Maureen Peters, Secr.

1987
Jan Redick, DC
Sharon O'Brien, Jt DC
Mrs. Clay Teske, Tres.
Mrs. Reed Peters, Secr.

1988
Sharon O'Brien, DC
Linda Johnson, Jt DC
Mrs. Clay Teske, Tres.
Mrs. Reed Peters, Secr.

1989
Sharon O'Brien, DC
Sue Bender, Jt DC
Mrs. Clay Teske, Tres.
Carol Zorb, Secr.

1990
Julie Atwood DC
Marlene Beatty Joint DC
Carol Teske, Treasurer
Ann Conzemius, Secr.

1991
Julie Atwood DC
Marlene Beatty Jt DC
Maureen Peters, Secr.
Chris Doxan, Treasurer

1992
Julie Atwood DC
Marlene Beatty Joint DC
Faye Hobley, Secr.
Debby Irwin, Tres.

1993
Dr. Nancy Perry, DC

Faye Hobley, Secretary
Debby Irwin, Treasurer

1994
Penny Sophir, DC
Sue Stratta, Jt DC
Elizabeth Donelson, Secr.
Fay Hobley, Treasurer

1995 - 96
Susan Stratta, DC
Penny Sophir, Joint DC
Barb Fishman, Secr.
Anne Perlebach, Tres.
1997
Susan Stratta, DC
Penny Sophir, Jt. DC
Barb Fishman, Secr.
Patrice Urban, Tres.

1998
Barb Fishman, DC
Judy Brown, Secretary
Patrice Urban, Treasurer

1999
Barb Fishman, DC
Patrice Urban, Jt DC

2000
Tim Waters, DC
Barb Fishman Jt DC
Karen Furst-Meeks,
Secretary

2001
Sue Hull Jt DC
Debbie Tomek, Tres.

2002
Susan Sucha Hull, DC

Judy Bell, Jt DC
Kristen Gottschalk, Jt DC
Annick Smith, Secretary
Debbie Tomek, Tres.

2003
Susan Sucha Hull, DC
Judy Bell, Jt DC
Rhonda Robbins, Secr.
Debbie Tomek, Tres.

2004
Susan Sucha Hull, DC
Shari Parys, Jt DC
Rhonda Robbins, Jt DC
Debbie Tomek, Tres.
Liz Neary, Secr.

2005
Susan Sucha Hull, DC
Rhonda Robbins, Jt DC
Debbie Tomek, Tres.
Liz Neary, Secr.

2006
Susan Sucha Hull, DC
Carla Conroy. Secr.
Liz Neary, Tred.

2007
Susan Sucha Hull, DC
Katharine McLeese, Jt DC
Beth Delano, Tres.
Angela Davidson, Secr.

2008

Susan Sucha Hull, DC
Katharine McLeese, Jt DC
Beth Delano, Tres./Secr.

2009
Katharine McLeese, DC
Beth Delano, Treasurer
and Secretary

2010
Katharine McLeese, DC
Beth Delano, Jt DC
Mark Drabik Secr./ Tres.

2011
Katharine McLeese, DC
Beth Delano, Jt DC
Mark Drabik, Jt DC
Suzanne Rasmussen, Secr.
Pamela Knutson, Tres.

2012
Beth Delano, DC
Theresa Heye, Jt DC
Brenda Schmidt, Secr.
Liz Franzen, Tres.

2013
Sue Hull, DC
Beth Delano, Jt DC
Brenda Schmidt, Secr.
Liz Franzen, Tres.

2014
Sue Hull, DC
Pam Krecek, Jt DC
Sandra Fossum, Jt DC
Brenda Schmidt, Secr.
Liz Franzen, Tres.

Ponca Pony Club A and B Ratings by Year

1968 B
Jan Mactier
Debbie
McKinnon

1969 B
Nancy
Zandbergen

1970 B
Gretchen
Hennecke

1971 A
Jan Mactier, Jody
Moreland

1972 A
Debbie
McKinnon

1973 B
Patti Miller
Sharon Naughton
Jim Urban
Warren Weiner

1974 B
Tammy Cudahy
Stacy Godfrey
Jon Ketzler
Stephanie
Noonan

1975 B
Beth Maenner
Sue Gidney

1975 B
Valerie Grauer
Sue Martin
Jan Salestrom
Nina Cudahy

1975 A
Jim Urban
Janalee Salestrom

1977 A
Sue Martin
Wilde,
B Kay Salestrom

1978 A
Jim Urban

1979 A
Sally Lindwall

1981 B
Nina Cudahy

1982 A
Kay Salestrom

1983 B
Leslie Hansen
Hillary Horner
Jane Kasner
Elizabeth
Lamphier
Krystal Seitzinger
Sandy Smalley
Kirstin Wagner
Lisa Yanney,

1983 HA
Sally Lindwall

1983 A
Janet Lynch

1984 A
Lisa Yanney

1986 A
Krystal Seitzinger

1988 B
Jaymes Salestrom

1988 HA
Elizabeth
Lamphier

1989 HA
Jaymes Salestrom

1990 HA
Shelly Lynn
O'Brien

1992 A
Kim Peters
Jaymes Salestrom
Lisa Teske

1992 B
Jennifer Beatty
Laura Perry
Lisa Hinde

Ponca Time Line
Events, Instructors, Clinics, Boarders, Horses

1965 – 1970
1957 Mactier family moves to North Post Road
1964
- Mactiers purchase land for Ponca Hills Farm
- North Hills Hunt started

1965
- Ponca Hills Barn built
- Jan Heads to Ethel Walker Prep School
- First Summer Camp - Mike Blose enrolled as 8-year-old.
- Beth Maenner and Allison Latenser in first camp
- Ann Mactier starts Ponca Hills Riding Academy

1967 Ponca Pony Club founded
1965-68 Omaha Charity Horse Show
1968 Allan initiates New Year's Day Ride, later Dr. Zhivago Ride

Instructors

Ann Mactier
Sally & Corey
Gaucasana Queal (1965 - 1990)
Ann Shepherd
Hans Post
Tom Ordway
(1969-1972)

Rick Eckhardt (1966-1971)
Kay Buchanan
Alex Adam
Gretchen Hennecke
Sue Martin
Deb McKinnon

Some Borders

Beth Maenner,
Charlotte Schenken
Dorie John, Andrea Steenburg
Don Dunn
Dr. Ted and Jim Urban
Eleanore MacDonald
Gretchen Giltner
Jean Mergens
Joan & Gretchen Hennecke

Karen Wahl
Kathy & Susie Armstrong
Kathy Bohi Wilson
Merrilee Hansen
Nancy Zandbergen
Pat Rothe
Patty & Susie Miller
Sharon Naughton

Bud & Stacey Godfrey
Stacy Truesdell
Susie Blackwell
Tom Caniglia

Cudahy: Tony, Tina,Tammy,
Hope and Nina.
Warren Weiner
Mindy Nance

Some Horses

Alibi Bart - Hennecke
Bliss - MacDonald, Ponca
The Barrister - Dunn
Chipmunk - Maenner
Cocoa - Cudahy
Dolly - Mactier
Eeyore
Happiness Is - Cudahy
Hireath - Ponca, Weiner,
        Dahlke

Invincible – Mactier
Linus - Schenken
Mr. Red - Mactier
Panache - Armstrong
Platte Black - Hansen
Van - Mactier
Tiffany Way - Naughton
Jenny Jones - Rothe

1970 – 1980

1972 Glenn Cudmore and family move to Omaha from Regina
Canada to manage Ponca Hills Farm with Ned Tennis
1973 U.S. Pony Club National Rally at Ponca
1972 Jan's horse, Christopher Robin, loaned to US Olympic Team
Mid 70s
  • Allan breeding Thoroughbreds at Ponca
  • Jim Urban Established Northern Hills Riding Academy at
    Ponca
1976 Robyn Carmichael and Jack Eden married at Ponca.

Instructors

Alex Adams
Ann Shepherd
Carole Cudmore
Glenn Cudmore

Jan Mactier
Kay Buchanan
Merrilee Hansen
Rick Eckhardt

Sally Queal
Sue Martin
Tom Ordway
George Schneider

Some Boarders

Bob Hanson
Charlotte Schenken,
Dorie, Andi & John Steenburg
Gwen, Amy and Sue Madison
Jim Urban
Judy & Rick Marshall
Kathy Armstrong

Lindy Stratbucker
Marshall
Merrilee, Leslie, Sara Hansen
Robyn Carmichael/ Jack Eden
Stacy Truesdale
Karen Theisen

Some Horses

Bambi - Cudmore
Becky
Jenny Jones - Rothe
Patsi

Sweeping Cloud – Hansen
Cinnabar – Theisen
Panda - Theisen

1980 - 1990

1981 Tom Ordway Marries Debbie McKinnon at John Grasmick's farm in Seward.
1983 Sonic Lady foaled
1986 Sonic Lady European Filly of the Year
1987 Wedding of Jan Mactier and Mick Moriarty

Instructors

Ann Carter
Dee Hudson
Jack Mosley
Jan Mactier

Linda McClaren
Sally Queal
Tom Ordway
George Schneider

Some Boarders

Anne Dolan
Beth & Lois Schrager
Bruce Rhode
Charlotte Schenken
Jane Kasner
Kathy Armstrong
Linda Gordman
Lisa Yanney
Margie, Elizabeth Hoffmaster

Pat Rothe
Stacey Truesdale
Susie Gordon
Vicki Krecek
Karen, Amber & Crystal Theisen
Darlynn Fellman
Larry Kavich

Some Horses

Beau Jangles
Cristabel - Hansen
Dixie Bell
Friendly
Jack Be Nimble
Joker - Johnson
Latigo - Tschetter
Lee - Dolan
Mercedes – Lanphier
Okay - Salestrom
Pat - Dolan
Piper - Rothe
Pumpkin - Salestrom
Sherman
Shilo
Snowman
Sophie - Tschetter

Sport - Ponca palomino pony
Sugar - Born at Ponca - Dolan
Sweet Caroline - Gordman
Trapper
Tulsa - Rothe
Webfoot (Pony who stepped
on everyone)
Whiskey - Thomas
Wimpy - Krecek
Wink – Rothe
Miss Margaret – Mactier
Maxie – Hoffmaster
Tamarack – Fellman
Oreo – Hoffmaster
Franchesca – Maur
Tristan – Theisen
Splash Dance - Schrager

1990 - 2000
1990 Jan presents 40 carrot shirts at picnic
1991 Fire at Ponca

Instructors
Amy Bender
Ann Carter
Bev Norton
Dee Hudson
Erin Cardea
George Schneider
Jack Mosley

Jan Mactier Moriarty
Linda McLaren
Lisa Laralde
Martine Marcelli
Melinda Redick
Sally Queal
Stacy Diaz

Some Boarders

Anne Dolan
Beth Schrager
Charlotte Schenken
Darlene Fellman
Gretchen Giltner
Jane Kasner
Jean Murphy
Karen Theisen
Larry Caniglia
Larry Kavich
Linda Bezdicek
Linda Gordman
Linda Johnson and daughters
Carrie and Tracy Johnson

Lisa, Mary, Charlie Roskens
Margie Hoffmaster
Mary Jessen
Mike and Fran Blose
Nancy Gordon
Pat Rothe
Pat Tschetter and daughter
Ann
Susan MacQuiddy
Tam Falvo
Vicki Krecek
Karen Theisen, Amber,
Crystal

Some Horses

Acid Test - Gordon
Butterscotch - Kavich
CynCyn - Krecek
Flurrie
Jake - Gordman
Lacey - Perry
Loretta
Moose
McKinley – Gordon
Oliver - MacQuiddy
Oreo - Hoffmaster

Pat - Dolan
Patch - Krecek
Rodeo – Kavich
Sugar - Dolan
Tamarack
Teddy Bear
Theisen/Schrager ponies:
Honey, Mr. Mahogany
Wink – Rothe
River - Hoffmaster
Stevie the Wonder Horse

2000 - Current

Instructors

Lisa Larralde
Stacy Diaz
Bev Norton
Erin Cardea
Martine Marcelli

Jack Mosley
George Schneider
Ann Wilson
Allen Wilson
Sam Lonigan

Billie Thone
Amy Bender
Natalie Shaw
Caleb Cooney

Ponca Clinics Over the Years

Ann Carter
Archie Cox
Arlene Rigdon
Bengt Ljungquist
Bill Coester
Bobby Dreyer
Kristin Bachman
Gabor Foltenyi
George Morris
George Schneider
Geoff Teal
Gordon Wright
Hans Senn

Jan Conant
Jessica Rigdon
Jim Graham
Jim Wofford
John Staples
Karen Healey
Karl Mikolka
Lady Mary Rose
Williams
Lisa Giltner
Lisa Jacquin
Lowell Boomer

Melanie Smith
Taylor
Michael Plumb
Mike Mathews
Michael Page
Michael Sosso
Ralph Hill
Rebecca Rigdon
Rick Eckhardt
Thady Ryan
Tom Ordway

Barn Managers

Ann Mactier
Sally and Corey
Gaucasana
Jim Mitchell
Alex Kemp
Rick Eckhardt

Glenn Cudmore
Tom Ordway
Ned Tennis
Dan McGuire
Steve Goodrich
Judy Csejthey

Gary Harnett
Jesse Harnett
Lenora Herd

Vicki Krecek

Figure 105. **The Author** Vicki Krecek introduces granddaughter Lauren to fox hunting. Here they wait for the Opening Hunt Blessing of the Hounds on her long time Morgan, Patch, at North Hills Hunt kennels, 2005.

Vicki Krecek was born wanting to ride horses. She learned to ride on invisible horses until her family moved to an orange and avocado ranch in Ojai, CA and she got a real horse. She loved English saddle and riding, often alone, in the rugged Los Padres National Forest. A Journalism graduate of the University of Nebraska, she married Dave Krecek, raised two sons, John and Mark, and had a career, first as a freelance writer and then at the Greater Omaha Chamber of Commerce. In the 80s, as a Trail Boss for River City Roundup, she rekindled her love of horses, took lessons at Ponca Hills Farm, and bought a horse in 1989. She has been a riding member of North Hills Hunt, Gamble Hills Hunt, and Fort Leavenworth Hunt and ridden hundreds of miles of trails in Nebraska, Iowa, Kansas and South Dakota. Still riding her two horses, Tessa and Ariel, she has given up the hard gallops across the fields, for trail riding and horse camping trips, all with good friends and great horses.

Other books by Vicki Krecek include:

Breaking Covert: An Early History of the North Hills Hunt 1964 - 1988 (Published 2011)

K 37472591 One Soldier's Story: U.S. Army Horse Cavalry - China -Burma-India Theater, 1943-1945 (Published 2013)

When, in 1965, Allan and Ann Mactier decided to build a barn as a center for English riding, their idea was to train young riders and support the establishment of a fox hunt in the Omaha area. Their enthusiasm, choice of a beautiful forested hilly acreage, and a determination to have the best instruction led to the establishment of Nebraska's first chapter of the United States Pony Club and the education of hundreds of young riders. Opportunities for training with Olympic level riders, riding cross country jumping courses, and fox hunting developed skilled riders, many of who have made a lifelong commitment to the horse industry. This is the story and the memories, of how it all happened.

Made in the USA
Coppell, TX
02 November 2019